The Power Look

EGON VON FÜRSTENBERG
with Camille Duhé

THE POWER LOOK

ILLUSTRATIONS BY RICHARD CHENEY

HOLT, RINEHART and WINSTON/New York

Library of Congress Cataloging in Publication Data

von Fürstenberg, Egon, 1946–
The power look.

Includes index.
1. Clothing and dress.   2. Men's clothing.
I. Duhé, Camille, joint author.   II. Title.
TT507.V65   646'.32   78–1995
0–03–020456–9

Designer: Joy Chu

Printed in the United States of America
2   4   6   8   10   9   7   5   3

To the man who encouraged
the writing of this book
by the example he set,
my uncle,
GIANNI AGNELLI

CONTENTS

ACKNOWLEDGMENTS

A special thank you to my many friends for their help, my family for their encouragement, my business associates for sharing their knowledge, and to Mary Blake, Diane von Fürstenberg, Judith Erlich, and Natalie Chapman.

Part I

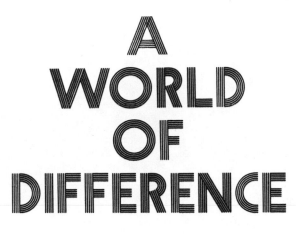

1

The Power Look

Why should a secure, intelligent man concern himself with clothing and the way he looks? Because it makes a world of difference. When I was about fourteen, my father, Prince Tassilo von Fürstenberg, invited a group of friends to his castle in Austria for a shooting party. I walked into a room where these men were gathered. Some had inherited titles and fortunes. Some had made fortunes of their own. Others were more famous than rich. Austrians, Englishmen, Italians, Frenchmen, and Americans were among them. I knew some of them well, others not at all. But in minutes it became clear to me—as I am sure it was evident to them—which men were really running things. There was something about the way they looked—authoritative, at ease, elegantly dressed.

Even earlier than that, as a young child, I often accompanied my parents to view various couture collections and absorbed the unstated codes of modern fashion and timeless classics. It was easy to spot the men of power by the clothes they wore and the assured way in which they moved. I used to watch the men coming out of the Rolls-Royces and knew even before I saw them that they would be dressed elegantly in clothing that always fit just right even when they were bending to get out of the car. That has always impressed me—clothing that continues to fit perfectly no matter what the body is doing.

Although styles have changed since then, that same look of relaxed assurance and mastery can be easily recognized on today's most important men, wherever they live and whatever they do. The real winners don't all look alike, but they do all have an unmistakable quality that can be yours.

My own awareness of the subtle messages conveyed by each aspect of a man's appearance has been sharpened in recent years through professional involvement. For my own company, and for a number of licensee firms, I design a range of menswear, from coats and suits through neckties, shirts, jewelry, and eyeglasses. I spend the days discussing design and production. I tour the stores and men's shops wherever I happen to be. Thus, I am constantly learning what works (and doesn't), what's available, and what's wanted by men all over America and Europe. At restaurants, clubs, and parties I study what men at the top are wearing and how they put it together. On planes I talk to other men about their businesses and mine to learn what they think about clothes and what they want from them.

That is how this book came to be written. I realized that what I have learned over the years could save time and money for other men. That the self-assurance and ease I have observed in the boardrooms and clubs, on the private jets and private beaches, wherever the powerful work and play, can be communicated and learned. And it's worth learning. The small investment of time and attention to your looks can pay off in substantially higher income and increased happiness.

Above all, clothing should be a pleasure, not a source of worry. What you wear should simply allow you to enjoy yourself more by helping you feel and look on top in every situation. The point of this book is to give you the means to forget concern over looking right or wrong, appropriate or inappropriate, and get on with the fun of dressing well.

The power look is a ticket to the winner's circle. It is a passport to the world where men enjoy privilege and pleasure, take command, and seem at ease everywhere. These men receive courtesies without having to ask for them. They get quicker and greater attention from waiters and clerks, more favorable looks from women; colleagues, clients, customers, and friends listen to them more readily because of their air of authority.

These consistent victories cannot be ascribed to clothes alone, of course. Professional and intellectual assets are obviously important, and an Einstein won't be held back by baggy suits. But in our society, appearances count. A lot. Clothes are 90 percent of our appearance. They are uniforms of affluence and power by which people are judged—like it or not—and the initial impression that is created with the right clothes is unquestionably influential in business and social success.

In the business world, discrimination by appearance is a fact of life. A friend who is senior partner in a prestigious law firm recently had to select one of four junior partners for an important out-of-town trip to complete negotiations on a major transaction with a client in Palm Beach. It was a great chance to shine. The man my friend finally chose, he told me, was "not any sharper than the other fellows, but he's the one who most looks as if he would be at home in that world." Unfair? Of course. But that's the way things work. What man has time to waste in being passed over for opportunities because he "looks wrong"? Especially when the right look is so easy to achieve, so quickly acquired.

Many men undercut themselves and cause others to undervalue them through rundown shoes, bad haircuts, and poorly chosen clothes. Often, it's because they think concern with their looks would seem effeminate. In fact, not caring reflects a fear of success, an unwillingness to compete with the top men.

Anyone can look as if he's made it, even while he's busy getting there. On his way up, a man has pressing financial responsibilities—mortgage payments, the education of his children, and so on. Yet, when he has extra money at his disposal he often considers investing it in a better, newer, or more expensive car, camera, or television set. Almost anything but a better-looking suit. He forgets that his clothes convey his achievements and self-respect to the world every day, even when his expensive skis are parked out of sight.

How can you learn all the subtleties that can enhance your

business and social life? You could spend a great deal of time in the world of powerful and privileged people, slowly deciphering the codes of their seemingly careless manner. Or you can spend a few hours with this book and absorb all those tricks I've discovered.

With the help of this book, you can learn to communicate power and derive pleasure through the clothes you wear. Everywhere in life today, the aim is to simplify. Here, you will find how to simplify investments and decisions regarding your personal style. This is a handbook to help you review your clothes and the ways of best putting them to work for you. It will give you the keys to finding that power style best suited to your way of life; and it will show you how to perfect the expression of your own style in the least troublesome, least expensive—and, I hope, most enjoyable—way.

Other specialists can tell you how to improve your golf swing, your sex life, and your business dealings. But what you can learn from me, and the use to which you put it in improving your major asset—yourself—can help even your golf game, love life, and career. It will certainly help you approach them all in a more confident manner. And self-confidence is the key to the power look.

2

Defining Personal Style

Before spending a dime on new, more effective clothes, spend a little time analyzing who you are and what you want to say through your clothing. In this chapter we'll consider how to find your own style and how to dress to suit it; we'll look at those factors, such as personal attitudes, local and national standards, and physique, that determine a personal power style.

The Importance of Personal Style

Standards vary from man to man, place to place. Since your aim is to look right wherever you go, remember this basic, most important rule of the power look: *Adhere closely to classic standards.* But also keep in mind this corollary: *Avoid die-stamp uniformity.* How to do both? Through personal style. No two people are the same, thank God, and it's the uniqueness of individuals that I feel makes life interesting. To be a carbon copy of the next man, no matter how impeccable that man's taste, is unsuitable, not only because you could not feel at home in someone else's clothes, but also because an original always has more authority than an imitation. Personal style is where the fun of dressing well comes in. Once you've learned the standard rules, adapting them to suit mood and personality becomes a pleasure and works to your benefit.

The man of style and the guy in the next office may both wear three-piece navy blue suits. The man of style makes his seem unique. First, because it fits him perfectly (I'll give you the ways to guarantee that with even the most inexpensive suits a little later), and second, because he puts an individual stamp on the suit through what he wears with it.

The standard formula with a navy suit goes: white shirt, blue-and-white tie. Fine. It's a crisp, classic combination. There are equally correct alternatives though—not flashy but perhaps a little fresher, or a little more in tune with how you feel on a particular day. Say, for instance, it's been raining all week, and you have an early morning meeting and need a lift. With the navy blue suit, you might choose sunny colors: a pale blue broadcloth or button-down oxford cloth shirt and a soft butter-yellow challis tie with a small red pattern. Or say you feel ready to tackle the world. With your navy blue suit, you could wear a white shirt with a pin collar, a burgundy-and-white stripe silk rep tie, and, if you like, a white or dark red pocket square.

The most ultraconservative offices sometimes maintain a white-shirts-only standard. Even there, you can display a bit of personality. My friend Tom is a banker with a very staid investment banking house. His closet is full of somber suits and white shirts. But he has—and wears—some of the brightest suspenders I have ever seen. Bright red suspenders can "inject a note of levity," as Tom puts it, into a very tense meeting in the boardroom. "I have found that when we get down to shirtsleeves, as these meetings eventually seem to do, everybody is tense and overconcentrating. And those suspenders work to relax the atmosphere. Somebody will kid me about them, somebody else usually asks where to get a pair, but it breaks the ice and works to my advantage, I find." A sense of humor in every occasion, I agree with Tom, is a must.

Colonel Serge Obolensky, my father's best friend, is an exiled Russian prince and R.A.F. flying ace who became the mastermind of the St. Regis Hotel in New York and, later, head of his own

Manhattan public relations firm. He has always been a model of masculine elegance. During his years at the St. Regis, he always wore the classic dark-suit–dark-tie power look, but with a twist all his own. Serge wore patterned shirts, but rather than everyday stripes, his fine white cotton shirts had widely spaced polka dots, bright red but no larger than the head of a pin. No monogram was necessary for those shirts to be unmistakably personal; they weren't startling, but they put Serge's own lively, individual stamp on the quiet suits he wore.

Van Johnson, the movie actor, is famous in New York for wearing fire-engine-red socks with an otherwise classic black-tie evening turnout. This gives an edge of dash on the dance floor and serves as a trademark, but doesn't clash with anybody's standards of propriety. A red shirt, on the other hand, would demand attention and so be irritating to others.

"Red" Adair is a brilliant and colorful Texan who can command a fortune for his unique services—saving millions of dollars by extinguishing seemingly out-of-control fires in oil wells with a special technique he has perfected. He has also perfected a way of expressing his specialty through clothing. He wears red enamel and gold cuff links in the shape of burning oil wells. You wouldn't be aware of them unless seated next to him as I once was on a flight to Houston, but once you notice the cuff links, you always remember him.

Each of these men expresses personal style in a different way. But as with every aspect of the power look, the element of surprise is always subtle, never jarring or unsettling. It's good manners in dressing.

To me, good manners consist primarily of putting others at ease in a seemingly effortless way. As soon as people become aware of the lengths you go to in order to make them comfortable, they become less so and your politeness becomes overbearing and aggressive. The right clothes work in the same way. They are never *too* impressive, but seem as natural and suitable to you as a tiger's fur is to him. In fact, you can even wear fur yourself and not seem ostentatious, but only if you see your fur as someting warm to put on and forget about. Stand there twitching in it, adjusting and showing it off, and others will sense your lack of ease. When your clothes really suit you, you stand still and move confidently.

Without suitability, there is no style. What is suitable for you depends on many factors, but I think the paramount one is your attitude. Mindset is even more important to personal style than physique is. Every man, no matter what his build, can have the power look. The old advice is that short men should wear vertical stripes to look taller. But the short man with a tweedy, casual style will not feel taller so much as he will feel locked behind bars in a three-piece chalk-stripe suit. Because his "visuals" are unsuited to his personality, he will project himself less forcefully, and maybe even seem *less* tall than he might in a medium-tone solid-color flannel suit that more closely fits his mindset. A big brawny man might think he should model his style on that of a football hero. But if his mind and activities are closer to those of, say, Ted Kennedy than O. J. Simpson, the extroverted clothes he wears will be incongruous and unsuitable. Rather than a force, he will seem an also-ran. You should always dress to suit the way you think and the life you lead.

Finding Your Power Style

In my late teens and early twenties, I usually dressed in what was considered "hippie" clothing. Later, as a stockbroker, I wore superstraight business clothing. Now that I've learned which styles and clothes work best for me and how to adapt appropriate business attire to my own tastes, dressing is always a pleasure—and an accurate reflection of me to others.

Our position and self-image improve as we go through life, but we are often slow to upgrade our clothing style accordingly. How do you really look to yourself? Does what you see reflect what you think of yourself? What you'd like others to think of you?

Once you've opted for the power look, the first step before adopting it is to reappraise the inner self. On the following pages is a mental style chart to help focus your thinking.

In every grouping of ten men, three or four have more in common with each other than with the rest of the group. The others may be peers in most respects, but not share the same tastes or outlook. You have certainly seen this "bonding" take place in your office, in your community, in your club. It is expressed in the ways and places these kindred spirits choose to live, in shared ideas and preferred ways of spending leisure time. It is reflected in the opinions others have of them, and clearly seen in the ways they dress. This is personal style all over again, but in a broader context.

There are as many personal styles as there are men, but only four major power styles. Every man who is in the center of life, rather than on the sidelines, belongs to one of these four groups. He has more points of similarity—regardless of his profession, age, or physique—with members of that style category than with men in others.

Look over the chart on pages 12–13. Select the power group that comes closest to illustrating how you see (or would like to see) yourself. Then, I'll help you put your own style to work for you.

You probably find that elements of your personality crop up in at least two of the groupings. Of course, no man is totally one-sided. But you will feel more closely allied to one form of expression than to the others. In projecting your true self through clothes, emphasize the major side of your personality. Take elements from the secondary grouping to assure individuality.

If you are predominately a Relaxed Classic type, it doesn't mean you should wear a ten-gallon hat like John Wayne's. It suggests, though, that in attitude and personality you are less formal than men in other categories. You will be happier than they would, and more yourself, in bolder, more rugged cuts, fabrics, and colors. In working out your own expression of the power look, you should lean toward those.

Throughout the book, I have grouped clothing suggestions according to their usefulness to men in each of the four mental-style categories. Always check your primary power group for the best bets for you. But to sharpen your sense of *why* it's right, look over suggestions for men in the other three groups. You will then develop an infallible understanding of what's individually right for you and what isn't. That will save you from ever making a bad buy again.

Another function of the chart is to point you toward those men

Style	*Personality Traits*
A. Relaxed Classic	Easygoing ... confident ... humorous ... extroverted ... outdoorsy
B. Conservative Classic	Firm and steady in his ideas and beliefs ... calm ... understated ... traditional
C. Elegant Classic	Restrained ... worldly ... quiet ... sophisticated
D. Adventurous Classic	Daring ... active ... self-assured ... a gambler ... gregarious

Seen by others as . . .	Usual Vacation Choices	Exemplars
"A good guy despite his success and money."	Woods, mountains, unspoiled places	Alan Bates, Marlon Brando, Jimmy Carter, Peter Gimbel, John B. Kelly, Jr., Steve McQueen, Ryan O'Neal, Robert Redford, O. J. Simpson, John Wayne
"The man to watch, he can do great things. And you can trust him."	Places for rugged sports—skiing, sailing, etc.—with lively people around	Julian Bond, Carter Burden, Dick Cavett, Walter Cronkite, Henry Ford II, Edward M. Kennedy, John V. Lindsay, George Plimpton, Elliot Richardson, John D. Rockefeller IV
"A true aristocrat."	Restful but luxurious resorts with every amenity	Gianni Agnelli, Hardy Amies, Fred Astaire, Earl Blackwell, Bill Blass, Peter Duchin, Douglas Fairbanks, Jr., John Fairchild, Cary Grant, Kenneth J. Lane
"He always makes things happen. Where does he get the energy?"	Cities or resort areas with lots of people and action	Muhammad Ali, Burt Bacharach, Warren Beatty, Harry Belafonte, Tony Curtis, Alain Delon, George Hamilton, Joe Namath, Geraldo Rivera, Richard Zanuck

The power look is expressed in four style groups suggested here: Relaxed Classic (top), Conservative Classic (bottom), Elegant Classic (left), and Adventurous Classic (right).

who may serve as guides to your self-expression. They can save you time and money, too. Most are highly visible public figures. Some have had expensive professional advice in achieving an image that sells. All are aware of the value of the power look. Next time you see one of these representatives of your style group, whether in a photo, on television, or at the next table, study what he's wearing and how he puts it together. Notice how his public image conforms to your own.

Most often the big difference you will notice is how clearly his statement is made. If you study old photos of any public personality, you can usually trace an evolutionary process. This is especially true of politicians who begin in small towns and rise to national prominence. Remember when President Ford discarded his boxy, brown plaid suits for trim, crisp navy blue and white during the 1976 campaign? Photos of President Carter in suits as the young politician from Plains, as governor of Georgia, and then as President of the United States show this evolution in progress. Why waste time with middle stages? Aim for the top.

Studying All the Options

As you involve yourself with your own style, you will find ideas for clarifying it all around you. As your interest grows, you will discover previously "hidden" avenues and sources of self-expression.

Take notice of those men in your business whose version of the power look comes closest to your own intended one. Observe how they meet needs similar to your own in the kinds of shirts and shoes they wear, the length of their hair. The nature of your business also affects your style choices. Bankers and lawyers, for example, tend to dress much more conservatively than men in other professions, probably to enhance their credibility. Men in more creative lines, like advertising, design, architecture, or publishing, have much more leeway; their clothing ranges from ultraconservative to dressed-up blue jeans. Salesmen usually do well to fit in with, but not upstage, their customers.

Get a reading on what's right for your own community. Accurate barometers of local masculine style can usually be found in the clothes of the man who publishes your newspaper, the one who owns the television station, the director of the museum, the president of the board of trustees at the hospital, maybe the chairman of the board of the local symphony committee. Look at what they wear, then gear it to your age group and income level.

Glance through features on men's clothes and grooming in newspapers and magazines, especially those that feature "personalities" in their own clothes. Fashion editors work with great taste and flair to show you the wide variety of things available to you, but as they are primarily concerned with fashion news and creating lively photos, it's not always wise to buy according to this month's issue. It is important, though, to know the general direction of style—as opposed to the tricky, mercurial "latest fashion"—to avoid looking stuffy. Lapels, trousers, and neckties all widen and narrow in slow, cyclical movements. By glancing through the magazines, you can judge how the wind is blowing and be better able to stay current without buying new clothes every month. Look, then decide—and *always opt for the more conservative*. The most influential men are invariably slightly more subdued than those below them in the hierarchy. When it's a choice between the bright red tie and the burgundy-colored one, pick the darker color.

Where You Live Affects What You Wear

Today a certain universality in clothing is becoming more and more the rule. The well-cut navy blue suit, no matter where you buy it, looks authoritative almost anywhere you wear it. But certain regional considerations and preferences still apply. When you buy your clothes, consider not only the standards of your home town but also the extent and nature of your business and pleasure travel.

On his home ground the Bostonian looks and feels secure in a three-piece midnight blue chalk-stripe suit. In Phoenix or Houston, though, it might seem too formal, too drab, "too much." So headed for the Sun Belt on business, that northeasterner would leave the blue chalk stripe at home. Instead he might take a solid navy blue, a medium gray, or a tan suit. On the plane he might wear his navy blazer with tan or gray trousers. Instead of dazzling white shirts, maybe soft blue or cream-colored ones, along with a few lightweight turtlenecks or polo shirts, since in the Southwest it is more common to go without a tie after hours.

If you are from the South or the West and headed for Washington or New York, pack your darkest suits and lightest shirts—things that reinforce a crisp, conservative image. The light colors and lively patterns that appear to good advantage under a big western sky or a soft southern one can seem garish in sooty northeastern cities.

My friend George Plumbridge lives in New York and works in an advertising agency. He wears dark gray and blue suits into the home office, but his major account is a big furniture manufacturer in North Carolina. He flies down there regularly for meetings and keeps a few suits in his closet especially for those meetings: subdued glen plaids and solids that are much lighter in color and weight than anything he wears in New York. It makes sound business sense, George believes, to dress according to your surroundings, and in the South men do wear lighter clothes. "Besides," he says, "I enjoy the change."

Generally speaking, the farther north and east in the United States you go, the darker the colors worn and the more conservative the styles. Epicenter of this is the Boston–New York–Washington megalopolis. Granted, New York can also be one of the least conservative American cities, but not in the downtown financial district or in the midtown offices of the major corporations.

Color and pattern get lighter, more exuberant, more relaxed as you travel south and west. Men in Chicago and Atlanta wear medium gray more often than their counterparts in New York and Boston, who tend to prefer darker Oxford gray. Plaid business suits are worn more outside the Northeast. South of Atlanta and west to Los Angeles, appropriate colors are considerably clearer and paler.

Now, here are some special cases.

Texas. The Lone Star state has a power look of its own. A well-dressed man in Dallas may give his suit a twist of regional style by wearing fine western boots with it. He may add a big-brim Stetson hat. To eastern visitors this city-slicked cowboy style looks very dashing. Almost every man who goes to Texas wants to take away a pair of western boots. The easterner visiting in Texas will do better, though, to wear his usual style, but less formal and in lighter colors. By the same token, the Texan's powerful style may look like a costume in New York. The smart westerner in the East doesn't flaunt his $300 embroidered lizardskin boots and creamy white ten-gallon hat. That looks corny to New Yorkers.

Hawaii. Just as Hawaii is outside the continental United States geographically, it also stands somewhat outside mainland standards of the power look. I would suggest that a man in Honolulu forget gray suits and wear tan instead. Gray never seems to look good to me in the tropics (Florida included). Navy blue looks great, though.

New York. The city goes to extremes: very conservative suits for conservative businesses, or the most casual (but fashionable) clothes for more creative professions or for going out at night. But nothing in between. For most of the country, the "leisure suit" is seen as an acceptable, if unattractive, alternative to a real suit. Not in New York, though. NO LEISURE SUITS is the message on a placard stating dress rules at the fashionable Windows on the World restaurant at the World Trade Center. Same at Régines, the exclusive discothèque. At the most glamorous New York parties and openings men wear black tie or they wear jeans and velvet jackets with turtlenecks or open-necked silk shirts.

San Francisco. In its dress standards, as in so many other ways, San Francisco is unique among American cities. Here the most conservative "Old Guard" look is the best.

Los Angeles. L.A. is a problem. Full of flowers and palm trees, in spring it is as colorful as a fiesta. The Beverly Hills Hotel is set like a big pink resort in the middle of a semitropical park with tennis courts and swimming pool. The Bel Air Hotel is even more like a resort. Having heard about the casual L.A. life and the balmy weather, a man planning a trip there might think of taking resort and light, summery clothes. But, at the chic Beverly Hills restaurant, the Bistro, or at lunch in the private California Club, he can feel very out of place in a white linen suit. Other men will be wearing suits as dark and discreet as any found on Wall Street. At six o'clock, he must wear a tie to drink in the garden-facing Polo Lounge of the Beverly Hills Hotel. Best daytime clothes for Los Angeles are medium-tone—tan, blue, or gray suits, or a navy blazer and tan trousers. There's no question, though, that L.A. men are more casual at home and at parties than New Yorkers. Especially the hosts. Harold Robbins and his wife once gave a very big party which I went to in black tie. The host greeted his guests in silver-studded jeans and western jacket made of sky-blue suede. I felt very overdressed until I noticed that about half the guests were in black tie; most of the others wore either light tan suits, like James Coburn's, or blue ones, like Fernando Lamas's. Warren Beatty looked particularly together—casual but well dressed—in a black velvet jacket, open-necked cream silk shirt, and cream gabardine pants. (That combination would work just as well in New York.) At the regular dinner and movie screenings on Sundays at his huge Playboy Mansion West in Holmby Hills, Hugh Hefner wears a terrycloth jump suit. Everybody else wears blazers or sports jackets, some with a tie, some with turtlenecks, others with open shirts. You never know in Southern California, but with a dark suit, a medium-tone suit, and a blazer you are as ready as possible.

Her Opinion Counts

If you are fortunate enough to have someone in your life who really loves you, she is probably also your best friend and, therefore, usually the best advisor on clothes to enhance your appeal. She will know what the blue tie does for your suit and for you, as well as why the rust tie is wrong for both. She can give invaluable suggestions about the best colors for you and how things should look and fit in order to present you at your most good-looking.

You should adapt her ideas to the real demands of your situation, though. Say the question is one of buying a business shirt. She is along and suggests that, of the pale pink, pale yellow, light blue, and white, the pink looks best. Find out why. It may be that she has noticed you look healthier and your stubble of beard is less apparent at the end of the day when you wear something other than a white shirt. You may know or feel that the pink shirt won't go over well at work no matter how flattering it is. (In the most conservative businesses in America, pink is sometimes unacceptable—though I often wear it and think it looks good on all men; pink shirts are quite common, however, in England.) Rather than a flat veto of her suggestion, ask how she feels about the pale blue or yellow shirt. Both are acceptable, yet it may well be that one will look better on you than the white shirt you might have chosen on your own. It's always good to get another opinion, especially from someone who shares your desire to improve your looks.

When it comes to fashion *per se*, women frequently care more about men's fashion than men do. Surprisingly, 65 percent of all menswear is bought directly by, or in consultation with, a woman. She might be more likely to suggest the "latest thing" than your colleagues will be to accept it, however, so you should probably weigh her decisions carefully before buying clothing for the office.

For after hours, though, and the times when you will be together, buy whatever she thinks you look appealing or sexy in, as long as it's comfortable for you.

Although my wife, Diane, and I are separated, she is my best friend and closest advisor. I have always followed her suggestions when dressing for parties. Her taste is excellent, she knows immediately what looks good on me and what doesn't; and that rush that comes from mutual pride always adds to the fun of any occasion.

Physique

As I've mentioned, your mindset is more important than your physique when it comes to dressing with style. The clothes which best suit your personal style enable you to *feel* taller, trimmer—however you want to look—and to project that feeling to others. Still, clothes can serve to maximize or minimize physical assets and liabilities. The following suggestions about the visual illusions clothes create can be adapted to suit your style.

There are four different power style groupings, but only three

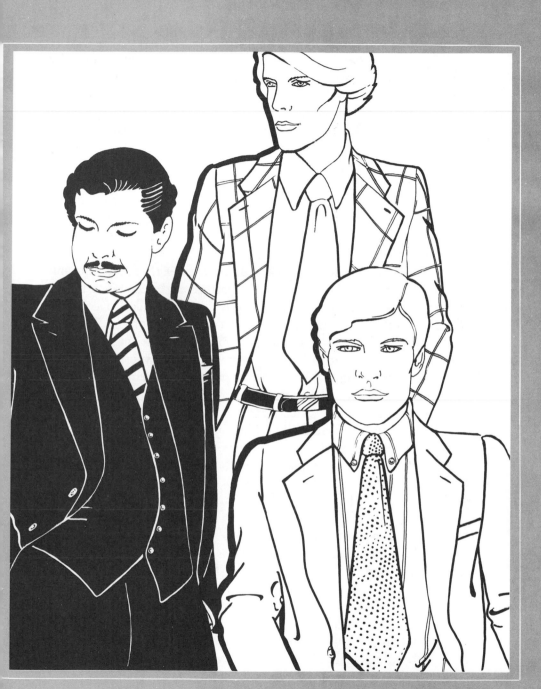

The endomorph, the ectomorph, and the mesomorph can maximize physical assets and minimize liabilities through the right clothing choices.

basic body shapes. These are: the *ectomorph*—tall, thin, long-boned, and narrow; the *endomorph*—thickset and inclined to fat, often the shortest of the three; and the *mesomorph*—in between, with what is called an "athletic" body. As with personality, every man combines features of more than one type but can be classified as belonging predominately to one category.

The long, lean ectomorph should remember that sharp contrasts between color of jacket and shirt or jacket and trousers are broadening . . . medium and light tones of a color make a man look shorter and stockier than very dark ones . . . a wider, brighter tie emphasizes the width of the face . . . wearing hair somewhat fuller at the sides suggests a wider face.

The heavyset endomorph should remember that shirts in white or pale color and ties with decisive pattern and deep color tend to draw the eye upward . . . smooth-finish fabrics in darker colors are more useful than fuzzy, tweedy cloths in light colors . . . the most eye-catching element of clothing should be higher on the body to draw the eye upward, so avoid fancy shoes and experiment instead with a white or bright-colored breast pocket handkerchief.

The mesomorph has the good fortune to be able to wear just about anything well. An exception is the mesomorph who is very tall and powerfully built. The "big bruiser" can easily intimidate other people, so he should tone down his size and threat (around other men, anyway—it may be a drawing card with women) by avoiding extremes of any kind and choosing soft, muted colors that blend in rather than contrast sharply.

Some tips if you are *too short*:
· Choose smooth fabrics
· Wear matching (or close) colors for jacket and trousers
· Wear trousers with plain rather than pleated front
· Investigate jacket styles that have a slightly higher waist
· Wear narrow belts
· Look for shirts that don't have a wide spread collar
· Choose smaller, rather than bolder, plaids if you wear them
· Medium tones are better than very light or very dark for suits
Some tips if you are *too tall*:
· Wear pleated pants
· Wear jackets with flap or patch pockets when you can

· Think about plaids when picking suits
· Look for fabrics with depth—flannel, tweed, or linen looks
Some tips if you are *too heavy*:
· Avoid roped shoulders; wear a natural shoulder
· Wear your trousers a bit wider
· Have set-in pockets on jackets
· Wear darker colors more often
· Pick small, allover patterns
· Choose matte textures over lustrous ones
· Don't wear anything too tight

3

Buying and Fitting

Now that you have some idea of your own power style, how should you go about getting the clothes to express it? In this chapter we'll consider how to shop and buy, and how to guarantee the best fit. The first step is to assess your current holdings and get rid of dead weight. Next, comb the best stores in your area to get an idea of the price and quality of what's available and to find a good salesman for your tastes and needs. Finally, learn the points to consider in getting your new purchases to fit perfectly.

Review Your Holdings

Don't spend any money until you've carefully assessed your clothing needs. You might already have most of what is right for your expression of the power look.

First, review the past with an eye on future needs. Like skull practice in football—running over all possible plays in a game so as to be ready for anything—go through the closet armed with your new information about your needs.

There is probably too much stuff. Most men own several suits and sports jackets that get them nowhere. Clear out the dead wood. The acid test is Times Worn. If you haven't worn it—tie, shirt, anything else—in the past year, you won't wear it in the next. A shirt that doesn't fit quite right, an unappealing tie—they don't have to be stained, torn, or outdated to be discarded. If they just never get worn when appearances count, get rid of them.

Men are often sentimental about clothes. Even the man who is invariably well turned-out is probably hanging on to four or five baggy, moth-eaten sweaters from his college days, along with a few pairs of threadbare pants. He usually rationalizes by saying that they're fine to wear around the house, while painting or working in the yard, when on the boat, or whatever. Unless you have half a dozen dirty work projects on tap, you don't need them. Just one pair of old, stained pants will see you through a whole year of grubby jobs. You have to be ruthless when it comes to getting rid of dead weight. I know it hurts. It may be almost traumatic at first, but you'll find it has a positive effect in the long run. There's something mildly depressing about keeping a lot of shabby clothes around.

Pull out everything you think you probably should get rid of. Lay it all out on the bed—neatly, so everything can be seen. Get a good visual fix on it. If it's not worn out, try to decide what's wrong with each thing. Then resolve not to buy anything like it again. Now get it out of your way. You can get a small tax break if you donate your old clothes to a charity thrift shop. Take advantage of it. If you have a couple of hardly worn sweaters, you might give them to a friend or relative, but as a general rule it's quicker and easier to call the thrift shop.

Now there should be space in the closet for things that do fit you and your new attitude. That's better for the clothes—they hold their shape better when not crushed together. It's also good because you can see right away what you have and what you need.

Check everything you have decided to keep. Does it need cleaning? Mending? This is the time to know about the loose buttons and broken zippers and have them taken care of. Dressing in a hurry for a meeting is not the time to learn that your trousers could stand a pressing. If you've ever knotted together a broken shoelace and hoped no one would notice it, you know what I mean.

The best way to redefine your appearance is to make a series of minor readjustments in it. It is not only easier on the budget, but also less startling. No man wants to be kidded or asked "Hey, what did you do to yourself? Trying to be a fashion plate?"

An example of how tricky this business of changing the image can be: Ned, a friend who was losing his hair, decided to have a toupee made. He was worried about eventual comments on his new "rug," so he began growing a beard. His friends and co-workers were, as always, fascinated by the progress, commenting on every stage of growth by saying how good he looked in the beard or advising him to shave it off. Ned counted on this and made the most of it, focusing attention further on his face and away from his head by asking how people liked the beard. Then he announced his plan to shave it off. When he went into work the next day, clean-shaven but with the toupee covering his bald spot, people studied his chin and told him how much younger he looked without the beard. Almost nobody attributed the rollback of years to the new hair on his head. That's the power look in subtle action.

How to Buy The Power Look: Prepurchase Points

Right now—having analyzed your desired projection of yourself and the current state of your holdings—you know whether you are in the market for a new suit, two suits, or a new pair of jeans. Throughout the book—especially in "The World of Business" and "The World of Leisure"—I will suggest those clothes I know to work best for men whose power look is similar to yours as well as how to combine them for the best effect. But the decisions are all yours.

Some men regard learning to acquire the right look as a game in which they can gradually become consistent winners. Most of us simply cannot afford to buy our clothes in the spirit of "win a few, lose a few." The stakes are too damned high, and we haven't the time or money to waste.

Sure, money helps everything. But in achieving a power look, attitude is even more important, preplanning is crucial, and self-knowledge is vital. Even if you have cash to spend, these tips can help you spend less for bigger returns.

That's why I strongly urge you to read the next section before buying anything, no matter what you have decided you need. Think carefully about how the projected purchase will advance your cause, and bear in mind the information on the next few pages.

Where to Buy

Even a medium-sized town offers more men's clothing outlets than it will pay you to visit. In a large city, covering all the options is simply a waste of time.

You can find the best store for you while having your morning coffee. Review the newspaper ads for the local men's stores. Study them as if you were new in town. Now, at the start of your campaign, have an open mind. Try to forget preconceptions and the past. It doesn't matter now that you've always bought in a particular store, or have a charge account there, or that it's near your office. It doesn't matter that you've never set foot in the store, either. Look at the ads—the kinds of clothes shown, what's said about them and how it's said, the look of the ads. It isn't easy, but try to ignore the prices. That isn't (for the moment) a consideration. Right now you should be looking only to decide which stores can best serve you in self-expression, which have the right personality for you.

You don't think a store has a personality? Think again. In retailing, store presidents come and go, advertising people are hired or fired, buyers are promoted or not according to their skills in projecting the image and personality of the store. What's bought and how it's promoted depends entirely upon store personality. The outlines of that personality are shaped according to the personality of the customer the store wishes to attract and keep. Every men's specialty store has a specific kind of man in mind. The best department stores have a somewhat wider base of appeal, yet they recognize that trying to be all things to all men will result in being nothing much to any of them.

The appeal of Brooks Brothers is so clearly defined and distinctive that the store name has entered the language. Even to people who have never set foot inside the stores, "a real Brooks Brothers type" indicates a certain socioeconomic standing, educational level, and outlook on life usually thought of as "Ivy League."

One Brooks Brothers store stands in New York at the corner of Madison Avenue at Forty-fourth Street. Paul Stuart and F. Tripler, two other fine men's specialty stores, are to be found within two blocks north of Brooks. All three share a reputation for superior quality and taste, yet each has a very different personality. When Abercrombie & Fitch was in business in the same area, you found four distinct stores, each making its major appeal to members of a different mental style group.

Brooks aims to be (and frequently is) home base for the Conservative Classicist, Paul Stuart for the Adventurous Classicist, and Tripler for the Elegant Classicist. A & F appealed to the Relaxed Classicist.

Each man can naturally find his needs met in other stores as well. Saks Fifth Avenue's personality is oriented mainly toward the Adventurous and Elegant Classicists, Bloomingdale's toward the Adventurous Classicist, and so on. When he travels, the Adventurous Classicist who buys at Paul Stuart, Saks, and Bloomingdale's in New York probably recognizes his personality reflected in such stores as Louis in Boston, Britches of Georgetown in Washington, D.C., and Mr. Guy in Los Angeles. Each has its own personality, but each is recognizable to him as the store most likely to have merchandise that has been carefully edited to attract him and to meet his needs.

TOO RICH FOR YOUR BLOOD?

You may know without thinking which store is best suited to the look you wish to project. Perhaps you have stayed away because it has a reputation as the most expensive in town. Forget it. For the moment, you should be shopping, not buying.

Price is too important to ignore. But the plain truth is that even the most expensive store stocks a certain range of prices. I once did some shopping for a suitcase and was surprised to find that the price of the kind of canvas bag I wanted was lower at

Gucci than at the "cheaper" store I went to first. That's not always the case, but you won't know unless you go in to find out.
At Saks Fifth Avenue the $500 suits and the $125 suits are sold on
the same floor and by the same salesmen. You can look at and try
on any or all of them, but you'll never know what bargains exist
in the expensive store until you check it out.

You might plan to go in when the store is having one of its
semi-annual sales. Every store, even the most prestigious, puts
fall and winter merchandise on sale just after Christmas or at the
first of the year. Around the Fourth of July is sale time for spring
and summer clothes. Selection is naturally somewhat more limited then than at other times of the year. However, since the store
that is aiming its appeal toward you probably stocks greater quan-
tities of things that suit you, chances are you will find something
you like and want there more easily at sale time than in an unsuitable store at any time of the year.

Find out in advance when the sale will be held. Going in
beforehand, you may be able to discover what is to go on sale and
have something set aside for you by your salesman. This isn't always possible, but often it is. It's certainly worth investigating.

"Just Looking, Thanks": How to Shop

First, just go in to have a look around at what the stores sell.

Assure yourself of the salesman's best attention and advice by
looking as if you're worth it. Walking into the store in your best
is the only way to walk out in something better. Too many men go
out to buy a business suit wearing sloppy lawn-mowing clothes.
Even if you are only going in to buy a sweater, go in "properly
dressed." A salesman is also a businessman, and he'll be more
disposed to spending time with and for you if you don't look as
though time is all you can afford to spend.

Aside from establishing an affluent image, there are other ad-
vantages to "establishment" dressing when checking a men's
store. One is that you needn't rely on memory. Say you need a tie
that works with the gray suit you have. Is it more blue-gray or a
brownish-gray? Not even an artist has totally accurate color mem-

ory, and a pink-beige next to a gray-beige can be ugly as sin. Wear the suit into the store if you want to be sure of getting a shirt or tie that goes with it. Another advantage to wearing a good suit into the store is that you and the salesman have a better idea of how your suits should fit.

Retail salesmen hear the phrase "just looking, thanks" in their sleep. You won't be the first man who's said it, so don't worry that you aren't in a rush to buy. You should be just looking now, even if you do want to buy a new suit soon.

Instead of making a line drive for the 40 Regulars hanging at the back of the store, amble through. Especially if you are unfamiliar with the store, look at the patterns and colors of the neckties and shirts, how things are coordinated in the displays around the store. Are what you've seen the things in which you would be comfortable? Not paying for them, wearing them—we aren't yet talking about price. Do you like the look? Examining the merchandise geared to men who think the way you do, even if they can pay more, gives you the criteria by which you can judge clothes in other stores. Until you know the hallmarks of the $25 tie, you cannot get the most expensive-looking tie that $10 will buy. At the higher price level you may have noticed a particular depth and richness of color, or the butter-soft quality of the pale colors, the crispness and small scale of the patterns. This is important training for the eye and makes this trip worth taking. Now, no matter how little you spend for it, you know what to look for in a tie or anything else you buy. You can spot the power look wherever you find it.

Next, look around and pick out the salesman for you. The one who seems most sympathetic and knowledgeable is the man who will probably be useful in saving money for you.

THE GOOD SALESMAN IS YOUR BEST ALLY

I believe in specialists. If I have a sore throat, I don't want an eye doctor. When it comes to specific advice about your clothing, I think you should speak to someone who spends his life dealing with clothes. It can be invaluable to have an established relationship with a top-notch clothing salesman. Be honest with him about your needs, what you want to spend, and he can serve in the same way your accountant or lawyer does—to protect your interests in the most effective way, because he knows how.

Salesmen probably look at and handle more suits and neckties in a month than even their most stylish customers do in a year. They *have* to be more aware of what distinguishes the best from the run-of-the-mill. We aren't talking about taste—his might not be yours, and it needn't be. What we are talking about is expertise. When it comes to clothing, a good salesman in a good men's store has it.

Once you have established a good relationship with a salesman, he will become your closest ally in developing your power look. You'll have the advantage of immediate and understanding service; he'll have the advantage of a repeat customer. Many salesmen keep mailing lists of their regular customers and will notify them when new merchandise for their tastes hits the store.

Some people will tell you the salesman is mainly concerned with moving the stock and getting his commission and thus willing to sell anything to anybody who can foot the bill. That doesn't make good sense in anybody's business. Whether you sell stocks or suits, you know that it's sound economics to cultivate a repeat customer. Sell a guy a lemon, and you've seen the last of him. You can kiss future commissions good-bye.

There is also the snob charge against salesmen in men's stores. You know, it runs "How can he know what I want when he doesn't go to the same places or see the same people?" As I said before, the taste and the clothes are up to you. A good salesman won't suggest something inappropriate, providing he knows what you need (back to being honest with him); but he probably does know, if he's a good salesman in a good store, what has been bought by some of the most important men in town, so he can steer you toward (or away from) something similar. Salesmen in the stores I have visited—probably 90 percent of the better ones around the country—seem more knowledgeable and more sensitive to their customers' needs than I would have thought possible.

But about making that sale, getting that commission. Sure, that's his goal. As I have said, though, he wants you to be pleased with the purchase and with his advice, and to come to rely on him. That's why he'd rather sell you the best inexpensive suit the store has to offer and have you come back later for something else than put you down and send you away because you don't buy the most expensive. Ask to see something within your price range.

Beware of False Bargains

When buying an automobile, the stripped version of the better model is a wiser investment than the loaded-with-options cheaper make. That bit of sound financial advice applies to men's clothes as well.

In establishing a power look within a sound economic framework, you are better off with the lowest-priced suit model from a quality store that fits your personality than with the "top of the line" model from a mass-market outlet. The store that makes its appeal to men of limited means must offer clothes that look to them as if they're "worth the money." On their limited-success terms, that usually means adding flash and gimmicks to make up for inferior quality. Flashy styling has no more place in your suits than does shoddy material.

Sure it's tempting to spend less for clothes, and a bargain is nothing to be sneered at. But be sure it really is a bargain.

My friend Richard is a real money-saver. At least, he thinks so. He wears what I call squint suits. You've seen them—if the day isn't too bright and you squint your eyes, he looks great at a certain distance. He gets his suits, he is always happy to tell you, at what the ads call "below suggested retail." Judging by the way they look, I wonder who would ever have taken the suggestion. It doesn't seem to matter to Richard that the color of his navy blue suit is a little purplish, or that the material seems stiff and shiny; not at that price. What would matter to me, though, and to any man interested in the power look, is that they fail to perform—he doesn't look good in them. Even worse, they require a hell of a lot of time to maintain. Because they are made of inferior materials, they need plenty of care to look passable, yet they still fall apart in short order. Richard's suits usually last no more than one year before getting worn and shiny, baggy and shapeless. If he were to spend the same amount on one good suit that he does on two or three "bargains," he'd find it would probably last him a good four or five years at least. Better one well-made, more expensive suit to rely on than lots of cheap squints.

The last time he crowed about one of his bargains, Richard had just found a cashmere turtleneck for $19.95. He stocked up at the discount store and bought "four for the price of one if I had bought it at Saks." There was the black one that started popping at the seams the second time he wore it, and the gray one that was so badly stitched together at the waistband that it has to be tucked inside his pants to be wearable. He might wear the red or the blue—under another sweater or beneath a jacket—unless, of course, he's thrown them all away by now. He could have had one terrific sweater that would look good and hold up for years, but Richard likes variety and bargains. Who can afford them at that price?

It might have been in the window of a grocery or shoe repair shop, but I once saw a display card with a motto worth remembering: QUALITY IS REMEMBERED LONG AFTER PRICE IS FORGOTTEN.

That chimes with something I have finally learned: If you buy what you really want and will be content with today, you can be spared the time and cost of replacing it with something better tomorrow.

Cost-Cutting Points to Consider

· Never skip a sale at your favorite store. Even if you don't need replacements for your wardrobe, you may be able to make a killing in the market with shirts, ties, even socks that will cost less now than later in the year when you will need them. Pay special attention to the basic, go-with-anything white shirts, solid color ties, and such.

· When shopping discount stores and job-lot outlets, look for the stuff from which the labels have been cut out. It isn't a guarantee, but chances are these come from better-quality manufacturers and retailers who were forced to sell off good merchandise at a loss in order to free stockroom space for the next season's goods. Look closely, though, to make sure they weren't seconds—or worse, bad ideas from the beginning, like bicentennial celebration ties.

· If you have to cut costs somewhere, consider doing it from the skin out. Comparison-shopping the least expensive socks and underwear may indicate one way to save money without losing face.

· Investigate the maintenance requirements before buying anything. In their book for women, *Cheap Chic,* my friends Carol Troy and Caterine Milinaire call it "cost-per-wear." How many wearings, over how many seasons, with how many trips to the dry cleaner's is this garment likely to give? How long will you be able to wear it? The initially costly thing may turn out to be cheaper in the long run than the bargain.

The Way It Should Fit

"The jacket's too tight" is a frequent complaint in men's stores. The complainer is usually a young man just moving up the ladder into better-tailored, higher-priced clothing.

He's used to cheaper suits, cut to allow enough freedom of movement to change a tire or play baseball while wearing the jacket. All that slack fabric and those boxy lines are precisely what make a cheap suit look cheap.

Good suits aren't skimpy or skin-tight either. But they do follow the natural line of the body more closely.

A man may balk at a jacket with a higher armhole or a narrower and more elegant cut to the sleeve simply because it doesn't feel as roomy and familiar as his old bathrobe. He is ignoring the fact that his suit isn't meant to look like a bathrobe. He should notice how much taller, more self-possessed the well-tailored suit makes him appear.

Otherwise, he simply delays achieving his goal of looking better in his clothes. He also misses the fun of having something with a new and better look, of being noticed in a new, more admiring manner.

The basic mechanics of a quality jacket demand that the chest is tailored in a balance with the upper back. Better clothes have less leeway through the chest (so they won't gap in front or ride up above your neck when you sit), and the entire jacket fits closer to the body as a result. In cheaper clothes the chest and upper back are cut fuller so that more men (whose bodies may be very different in shape) can wear the same size. Only a few of them will be well fitted, but life is easier for the volume manufacturer who can cut an almost unlimited number of identical jackets.

Make this practical, on-the-spot study in order to understand fit in the only way that counts—on you: Try on the highest-quality suit the store has in your size. Study yourself in it, notice the way it feels across the shoulders and through the arms; look in the three-way mirror to see how flat it lies across the back. Remember that. Even if you don't intend spending "that kind of money," you should know what it buys. Having tried the best, you will be better able to achieve the best look at any price.

What to Tell a Tailor: All About Alterations

A good ready-made suit can look better than a custom-made one, or it can look as if it were borrowed for the occasion. It all depends on the demands the buyer makes when the suit is being altered.

Meticulous attention to the fit of your suit will raise the initial cost. Tailors are skilled craftsmen, and their time is valuable. Still, if a suit is worth buying in the first place, alteration fees are a minor expense.

Because the alterations are so important, though, many men I know even tip the tailor who makes them. A $10 bill seems a small price to pay for a perfect fit for years.

Naturally, not every man needs or wants to spring for a big charge for alterations. If you are close to a standard size (most people are), you may be able to get total satisfaction and a perfect fit gratis in some stores, at a minimal cost in others. Many of the best stores offer alterations at no extra charge.

If you're in a hurry for a suit, you may be able to save some time and money by taking the suit away with you without alterations. Often, a neighborhood tailor or even a first-rate dry cleaner with an alterations tailor on the premises can make the necessary corrections in fit of a suit more quickly and less expensively than would be possible in a large store where the alterations department is swamped with work. If you decide upon this course of action, you should ask whether the store offers any discount for forgoing alterations. This may very well be the case in stores that do not charge for routine alterations.

The perfect fit: (a) smooth across back; (b) vest fits like a glove; (c) cuff shows one-half to three-quarters of an inch; (d) smooth across front; (e) jacket sleeve ends five to six inches from tip of thumb; (f) trouser button covers navel; (g) cuffed trousers fall parallel to floor; (h) uncuffed trousers slope down in back.

Whether you're in the store where you're buying the suit or at your own tailor's, wear the shirt, tie, vest, and trousers of your best-fitting suit when having the jacket of a new suit fitted. These should all fit perfectly, exactly as you want the new things to fit. You and your tailor now work from the outside in, and from the top down.

JACKET

First, put on the suit jacket. The crucial, most often overlooked area of fit is the neck and the expanse across the shoulder blades. The jacket must lie completely flat across them. The chief hallmark of the ill-fitting suit is a small buckle, fold, or pull across the back. This hunchback effect is all too common, easily noticed when a man sits down and his jacket rides up in back. This won't happen if the problem is taken care of now. Put on the jacket, then hunch your shoulders, raise your arms and lower them, and shrug your shoulders. The tailor should be standing behind you, and you should watch for trouble spots in the three-way mirror. If there is serious buckling perhaps the jacket is really the wrong size. If the problem is minor, the tailor will probably make a chalk mark for a tuck in the back of the jacket at the center seam. At this point, men are separated from boys. Ask him to show you the effect that tuck will have by holding the fabric while you repeat the arm-raising, shoulder-hunching act. It may well be that a tuck is all that is needed. Often, it takes more than that—and this is where the alteration fees can mount. For a suit to lie totally flat against the back, it is often necessary for the tailor to remove the collar completely, correct the center and seam, then re-attach the collar. You don't have to do this yourself to understand that it's a pain in the neck for the man who does. But it's your neck that's important in the suit you wear. So, if need be, insist. But be willing to pay and to wait for perfection.

Smoothness through the body is the next criterion. It's easy to achieve if nothing is carried in the pockets of a jacket. Italian men, often very vain about getting a slim look in their clothes, are willing to carry small bags for wallet, cigarettes, keys, pen, and other paraphernalia. I try to throw everything into the briefcase I always carry with me, but still wind up at the end of the day with pockets crammed.

When being fitted for a suit, be realistic. Keys, lighter, whatever you normally carry, should go into the accustomed pockets of the new suit. These things will wind up there anyway, so have the suit fitted to accommodate them. A good suit fits not only a man's body, but his life.

By the same token, the fitter's behest to "stand up straight" should not be taken too literally. It's good for the ego to show how tall you can stand, or how flat you can make your stomach. But later, wearing the same jacket, you will relax into your normal posture. If the jacket has been altered to fit you at your most soldierly, you may look ill suited when you're at ease.

At this point, it usually becomes apparent that one arm is slightly longer than the other, or one shoulder higher. For right-handed people, the right arm is almost invariably longer. A good tailor recognizes this, so he takes separate measurements for right and left sleeves (and for trouser length for right and left leg). Never worry about this kind of individuality. The alterations expert is there to make the suit fit you, not a mythical "ideal man." If he is good at his job, you will look ideal when he's done.

When it comes to length of jacket there is only one rule, but it is inflexible. The jacket must cover the rear end. When the style of the day is for a somewhat longer jacket, a man with long legs might want to try that. Fine, but never shorter than the point where buttocks meet top of thigh. This is checked while standing. Fit of jacket must be checked while sitting as well as standing. Button it and sit down. There should be no bulge or pull whether sitting upright or leaning forward in the chair.

The ideal sleeve length is up to personal taste. Men who like to show a lot of shirt cuff sometimes have jacket cuffs six inches above the tip of the thumbnail. More conservative men may want to edge it down to five and a half inches from jacket cuff to tip of thumb, but never closer than five inches.

VEST

Once the jacket is pinned and marked, take it off and check the vest.

The vest of the new suit replaces the one you wore into the store. It should fit over your shirt and tie as smoothly as a second skin.

TROUSERS

Trousers are fitted last of all. How they should fit is predetermined. The navel marks the exact point at which the waist button should hit. That is the Golden Mean. Button the trousers right over the navel, center the belt buckle there, and have the tailor provide a smooth, comfortable fit. Trousers should be barely loose enough for you to be able to slip the flat of your hand into the waistband. They should be just loose enough in seat and crotch for physical comfort and a smooth line when standing or sitting. Ask for the crotch to be pinned and taken in, if this is needed. Long in the crotch makes for a visual effect of old age and short legs.

Long in the leg, though, is fine. Have trousers tailored to fall straight down onto the shoe, almost covering the instep. Trousers without cuffs (serious business suits or anything for evening wear) should slope down in back and be up to three-quarters of an inch longer over the heel of the shoe. Trousers that will be cuffed (sportier suits or odd trousers) should hang parallel to the floor, as long and low as possible without a break. A break in the trousers breaks the long line of the leg. For most men, depth of the trouser cuffs looks best at about two inches. For a man whose legs are very long, this can be deepened somewhat.

It is not a bad idea to announce now that you may bring the suit back in a month or so for a few final corrections. These probably will not be needed, but suits sometimes do need them after being dry-cleaned and worn for a while. Be a bore. Insist on perfection. Establishing yourself at the outset as a serious customer may also guarantee a better job.

The Way to Save Money on Clothes

Taking care of clothes is the single most important factor in economizing on them. There are other ways—and they will be discussed later—but wear and care is always the major one.

You can be well dressed for long stretches of time with just two decent suits hanging in your closet. But they have to be hanging whenever they aren't on your back. If you come in and throw the jacket over a chair, the pockets crammed with junk, it's always going to look like hell. So will you. But if, when you remove a jacket, you also remove the things in the pockets, give the coat a shake to readjust the fiber, hang it up to air for a while, then put it in the closet—that jacket can be worn almost daily and almost indefinitely before it even needs to go to the cleaner's for a pressing.

After each chapter on each kind of clothing, there is a list of special care tips. If you follow them, you can save the cost of this book many times over. You will also guarantee always looking like a million dollars without spending it. And you will avoid the annoyance of discovering, at the last minute, that the tie you want to wear is too wrinkled for service—which is the kind of petty hassle an active man should never have to bother with.

Power in Action

Two last words before getting into specific suggestions about clothes for business, leisure, and travel. First, this book will tell you ways to adopt an external power look—that is, what clothing to wear to project the best image of yourself to others. It can't possibly tell you how to follow up the visual impression you create with appropriately matched behavior. That must, of course, come from you. But please don't think that projecting a look of power means acting pompous, ordering others around arrogantly, or displaying a wad of $100 bills. People often make the mistake of equating power with obnoxiousness or rudeness. There is no reason that personal power has to be gained at the expense of other people's feelings. Some of the most influential men I have known are also some of the most considerate. The power look is designed to project quiet command, good taste, and appropriateness for any occasion. The behavior to match involves good manners and an authority based on inner conviction that requires no display of unrestrained ego. The behavior is called savoir faire.

Finally, have fun with your clothes. Enjoy wearing them. Many men make it a point of pride not to be overly concerned with appearances. Often it shows, sometimes it doesn't; always they miss out on the pleasures that come from creative experimentation with clothing. If you have paid little attention to your attire up to now, you might feel self-conscious when first adopting a new style. That feeling is fleeting, and you will soon find yourself broadening your horizons in the kinds of clothing that give you pleasure to wear. Whether you set the standards of style in your community or haven't paid any attention to them until now, it is my hope that you will find information of value in this book, absorb it, and then take off on your own course.

Part II

THE WORLD OF BUSINESS

4

Suit Power

In the world of business especially, you are what you wear. Elsewhere, inappropriate clothes cost a certain degree of social security; in business, dressing incorrectly can jeopardize financial and even job security.

Fortunately, it is easy to dress well for business. Because the standards of corporate America are fairly strict, the rules are fairly simple. As the code is very slow to change, the right clothes are good long-term investments.

Blue-Chip Investments for the World of Business

Because my own early training was in economics and investment banking, I look at assembling the right clothes for business as the equivalent of assembling a sound investment portfolio. Begin with a small holding of blue chips, those suits that are to a working wardrobe what ITT, GM, and IBM are to securities—bedrock sure things. Then later, as needs and finances warrant, expand your holdings however you choose.

The blue-chip holdings every man needs for the world of business are a solid navy blue suit, a solid gray suit, a solid tan suit, a tweed (or tweedlike pattern) suit in medium grayish or brownish tones, and a tan raincoat with a detachable lining for warmth. That, basically, is it. To call this a basic wardrobe for the business world might sound dated, but to simplify your life is a modern goal. Owning a few well-chosen and perennially correct things that serve you well in all business situations is the best (and least expensive) way I know of to uncomplicate the business of dressing well.

Slight variations of cut and cloth will make these five items capable of meeting the visual and psychological needs of every man in every power grouping, right across the board. Review all four of the lists that follow to see how adaptable these basics can actually be. For example, the Adventurous Classicist of Group D may feel uncomfortable in a navy blue serge suit. For him the equally authoritative equivalent is the navy blue blazer jacket. When the basic blue-chip suit that's right for you is combined with a personal twist in assembling shirts, ties, and shoes to wear with it, you gain even greater individuality.

If any of the terms used in the following pages are unfamiliar to you, the glossary at the back of the book should clarify them.

FOR THE RELAXED CLASSICIST OF GROUP A

His attitudes, and possibly his surroundings, tend to be less formal than those of other men. To express his freedom, yet remain unquestionably correct for the world of business, he may want:

· Single-breasted styles. Since he probably removes his suit jacket when working, he should look for suits with matching vests to preserve a well-dressed look. For sportier situations, he may also want to own one or two nonmatching vests (in chamois suede, red flannel, or tattersall plaid, for example) to alternate with the matching vests.

· Bolder and more rugged fabrics.

· Medium tones and heathery blends of color for their somewhat less urban appearance. He should not be without one very dark suit, though, preferably navy blue.

The following suits are among the best choices for him in the world of business.

Blue Suit. Single-breasted navy blazer suit, with matching trousers and vest, of wool twist or hopsacking weave in a year-round weight. Navy worsted flannel or dark blue linen are other possibilities.

Gray Suit. Solid-color medium gray worsted flannel, worsted, or tropical worsted. An almost invisible shadow plaid in gray-on-gray, or a gray-and-white seersucker for hot weather are other good choices.

Tan Suit. Medium tan cavalry twill, whipcord twist, linen, or poplin.

Tweed Suit. Donegal and glen plaids in medium tones of grays, tans-and-grays, or tans-and-browns. Year-round tropical weights with similar tweed looks are also good.

FOR THE CONSERVATIVE CLASSICIST OF GROUP B

He is probably more interested than men in other groups in a low-profile expression of personal competence and reliability. He is unlikely to walk through the office corridors without his suit jacket, recognizing that he looks more in control when completely dressed for work. The cut of his clothes, and the fabric used, are apt to be softer and less constricting. For the world of business he might have:

· Single-breasted styles with matching vests, or trimly cut double-breasted models on occasion.

· Cloth that feels soft and luxurious but is durable.

· Solid colors, for greatest versatility, and only the most underplayed patterns, such as pinstripes or herringbones. His preferred colors are apt to be dark. To keep them from looking drab, he probably uses sharp, clean contrasts of shirts and ties in solid colors or traditional patterns in such quiet luxury fabrics as oxford and broadcloth, wool challis, and silk foulard.

The following suits are among the best choices for him in the world of business.

Blue Suit. Single-breasted suit with matching vest in solid navy blue worsted, worsted flannel, tropical worsted, or poplin.

Gray Suit. Charcoal gray single-breasted suit with matching vest in worsted flannel, wool flannel, or tropical worsted, solid or with white pinstripe or chalk stripe. Gray-and-white pincord is another possibility.

Tan Suit. Light or medium tone in cavalry twill, gabardine, or poplin.

Tweed Suit. Medium to dark tones of gray, gray-and-tan, or tan-and-brown in wool tweed or lightweight tweed effects. Herringbone and Glenurquhart plaids are also suitable patterns.

FOR THE ELEGANT CLASSICIST OF GROUP C

The operative word for his clothing is *crisp*. His bearing and attitude are equal to the demands of precise tailoring. Fit is a paramount consideration, and the fabrics and colors he prefers are usually as decisive as the style. For the world of business, he will choose:

· Trim double-breasted cuts when his build, and the weather, warrant. For all but the hottest weather, he most often wears a single-breasted suit with a matching vest.

· The most clear-cut patterns, but always in very neat, small-scale, or close color tonalities. Color preferences are apt to avoid the middle range—he usually likes a very dark, almost black shade or a very light one, worn with sharply contrasting shirts and ties.

· Fabrics with a smooth hand and clear finish. They may tend to be somewhat heavier in weight than those preferred by other men, because these heavier weights work best for the more structured suits he enjoys.

Among the suits he might choose for business are the following.

Blue Suit. Midnight blue or navy serge, gabardine, or tropical
worsted, single- or double-breasted cut. Tropical-weight navy blue
silk-and-wool blend in single-breasted style is also good.

Gray Suit. Single- or double-breasted dark gray unfinished worsted,
solid or with white chalk stripe. A dark gray tropical blend is also
suitable.

Tan Suit. Light tan single-breasted suit with matching vest in fine
gabardine or poplin. Ecru silk-and-linen blend is also handsome.

Tweed Suit. Single-breasted suit in Prince of Wales plaid or small
houndstooth check. A clear glen plaid combining light, medium,
and dark gray is another possibility.

FOR THE ADVENTUROUS CLASSICIST OF GROUP D

He expects recognition of his personal flair and vibrant energy;
he wants these qualities in his clothes. For admiration but not resentment of others in the world of business, he might decide on:

· Extra-special atttention to details of fit. This is more important than ever in the more up-to-the-minute styles he will almost
invariably prefer. The "latest" thing will look unimpeachably authoritative, but only when it fits superbly and is made of good-
quality materials and colors appropriate to the business world. He
probably prefers variety in cut, and wears both single- and double-
breasted clothes.

· Fabrics that feel and look as expensive as he can reasonably
afford. Unless his work world is as unconservative as his mindset,
he does better to stick to the wools and cottons of the world of
business than to get into velvets, corduroys, denims, and such for
his business suits.

· Colors that are becoming but appropriate. As for any man,
they should be true and rich blues, tans, and grays for the working

world. Fabric choices are often more textured, and in slightly bolder patterns.

Among the best choices for him in the world of business are the following suits.

Blue Suit. Navy blazer suit, double- or single-breasted with vest to match, of year-round weight in twill weave or wool twist.

Gray Suit. Single- or double-breasted soft gray-and-white pinstripe or chalk stripe. Other equally good possibilities are a medium gray soft wool flannel blazer suit, a medium gray or dark gray tropical worsted, a dark gray linen or linen look, or a shadow plaid in close tones of gray tropical worsted.

Tan Suit. Tan cavalry twill or light tan silk-and-wool or tropical blend. A fine tan gabardine, an ecru linen, or a camel's hair blazer suit are other good choices.

Tweed Suit. Small-scale pattern with dark and light tones of gray-and-tan or brown-and-tan in tweed or tweed-look tropical.

Color Considerations

Following dictates is a snap. Dressing for enjoyment and self-expression is a greater challenge. With the proper blue-chip holdings in suits and the right things to wear with them, you can do both. Just keep in mind this fundamental advice: *Dress by the rules, bending them to suit yourself.* But how far can the rules be bent? The available colors, patterns, and materials in suits are almost endless.

I believe that color is the keystone. Mistakes in style will be forgiven or even ignored if there is no mistake in color. A suit can fit beautifully and be made of the finest cloth, but if it's peacock blue the wearer won't gain as many points as if he wore a baggy suit in navy blue. *Unless you can give a definite name to the color, it's definitely wrong for business.* Purplish-blue, bluish-green, pinkish-beige, sort-of-orange, and similar hybrids are hard to name or describe with precision. They are almost impossible to coordinate successfully with shirts and ties. If you don't find exactly the right accessory, everything looks wrong, including the suit. Even if you do find the "perfect" dusty rose shirt or whatever, you risk looking too carefully "matched." For men's clothes, close-toning and matches look corny.

Aside from the obviously off-beat shades, there is another color that is best avoided for the world of business. Surprisingly, that is solid dark brown. Brown should have everything going for it; it's sober, quiet, and can look very rich. However, it alienates many people. The most spectacular instance is recounted by Andrew Tobias in his biography of the late cosmetics tycoon, Charles Revson. Mr. Revson, railing at a new executive for wearing a dark brown suit, shouted: "You know what brown is the color of, don't you?" and dismissed him from the office. (He was also very particular about his food. Every time I had him to dinner, his secretary would call a day in advance to order his menu—invariably steak and green beans.) Most people are not so voluble about it, but according to Faber Birren, the color consultant to the U.S. government and industry, "Few people like brown, but many dislike it." Skip it for your suits except as part of a tweed or plaid.

As you've gathered from the preceeding suggestions for blue-chip investments, there are only three fail-safe colors for business suits: true blue, from medium to midnight; gray, from smoke to charcoal; tan, from ecru to the color of a pecan shell. Mixtures of these, so long as they are in clean, true shades are also valid: blue gray, grayish-tan. These classic colors for business may sound constricting, too limited in range, but they actually offer freedom from concern over the most appropriate color choice. Alone or in almost any combination, these colors always look appropriate. And they offer freedom and ease of coordination when shopping or dressing—virtually any gray goes with navy or with tan. You can shuffle these colors together like cards and always turn up aces. They even offer guaranteed enhancement of your own looks—there isn't a man alive who doesn't look good in blue, for example. And, as you can see from the suggestions for blue-chip investments in the four power groups, these three colors offer a surprising amount of variety depending on cut, material, shade, and so on.

How Many Suits?

You're the only expert on how many suits you need. Base your decision on the business you're in, what men in your area wear for it, how much business travel is involved and where it takes you, how dramatic temperature and season changes are.

If you dress in a suit Monday through Friday, putting it on at seven in the morning and wearing it until seven at night, three suits is the minimum for a temperate climate. Each suit is thus allowed at least thirty-six hours of rest for every twelve-hour tour of duty. No suit should be subjected to more frequent wearing if it —and you—are to look the best.

How Much to Spend?

The smartest investments in business suits are made when you recognize that economy is not effected by the price tag alone. I'll repeat what I said earlier: Don't necessarily look for the most expensive suit in the store, but do use it as a standard for judging. You don't have to spend a lot to get a good deal. But purposely buying cheap is false economy for the world of business.

Not only do you look better at the outset in a quality garment, but it will look good for quite some time to come. In the world of leisure, style changes are frequent, and changes in your own attitudes toward your clothes may be even more rapid. Saving money on clothes you wear perhaps on weekends only, or at best for a couple of years, makes sense. But in the business world, it takes years for a suit to seem dated. Even then, in most businesses anyway, looking conservative is seldom wrong.

Because a better suit is better tailored and made of higher-quality materials, it usually holds its shape longer, if well cared for. Many "bargain" suits require a professional cleaning and pressing after each wearing. That's no bargain over the long haul.

Don't feel compelled to overspend on your suits. Follow the suggestions in chapter 3: Buy on sale, shop intelligently, consider all the angles for saving. Quality counts more than currency in the world of business. Buy your suits as if they were long-term investments, and you will get high yield for years.

How to Pick a Suit

Clothes sense involves—aside from common sense as to finances and needs—the sense of touch and sight.

The way the fabric feels to your hand is the acid test in selecting a suit. The professional term is *hand* or *handle*. Even before reading the fiber-content information on the label you should handle the fabric. All pure wools do not feel the same. Think of how a wool army blanket feels. Compare that to the touch of a lamb's-wool sweater. Not all polyesters have the same hand. Some synthetics are cold, clammy, and harsh to the touch. Others are excellent and feel as good as they look. Always trust your own touch.

More hand work before buying a suit: Squeeze the sleeve, hold it for a minute, then let go. If it springs back into shape, the suit is relatively sure to undergo periods of hard wear without serious wrinkling. If, after this brief trial, the sleeve remains crumpled, that's the way it will perform in actual wear, so it's a bad buy.

Sight is important, too. A trained eye seeks out those small details that characterize the quality suit.

Buttons. Buttons should look expensive, sewn on for keeps, and worth the effort in sewing. Even the buttons on your suit can reflect your style. On a navy blue suit, for instance, the man of Group A might prefer dark horn or tortoise shell; Group B and Group C men probably prefer buttons that more closely match the cloth in color and texture. The Adventurous Classicist of Group D often wants contrast between cloth and buttons and is happy with bright gold buttons against navy blue.

Metal buttons (as on a blazer suit), because of their thickness, tend to droop or hang a bit loose. No problem, but look for tight sewing nonetheless.

Pockets. Look for inside pockets of the number and kind you prefer. There should be one or two inside breast pockets. A button flap on these is a good safety idea, especially if you use a breast pocket wallet (I think you should for business). For maximum security the pocket could be closed with a zipper. Suits never come equipped with this detail, but either loop-and-button or zipper could be added to the suit during alterations.

Sometimes you find another inside pocket set in on the left side at about hip level. Because of its position, this small pocket is the ideal place to stash cigarettes and lighter. Whatever it holds, the placement prevents it from bulking out the line of the suit even when full.

Collar. Turn the collar of the jacket inside out to see the quality of manufacture. This is a standard test of the professional clothing buyer. He looks for a flat flannel lining, evenly sewn with small, neat stitches. This insures that the collar will lie flat against the neck and retain that shape through long wear and even abuse.

Lining. Look at the jacket lining. It should be silky smooth so there will be no tug or friction when you put the jacket on over your shirt or sweater. Color and pattern of the lining can be as brilliant or as somber as you like. The best material is Bemberg, a brand name for a synthetic fabric that is as smooth as silk but stronger and more durable. Tight sewing is extremely important in a jacket lining. Pinch a little of the lining cloth close to the place where outer jacket fabric and lining are joined. Pull gently and look for a row of very close-together little stitches. The smaller and tighter, the better.

In some very good suits you will find a triangular flap or inset at the base of the armhole. This may be of plain felt or it may match the lining fabric. This "sweat shield" will add greatly to the long life and good looks of a suit.

Hot-weather suits are usually unlined to be as lightweight as possible. At most they may have a partial lining across the shoulders and upper back. In this case, look for neatly bound seam edges inside the jacket instead of raw edges that can eventually unravel.

Trousers, too, are sometimes lined. This is done to prevent

abrasion that can shorten the life of more delicate fabrics, such as soft fine flannels. Some men also feel lined trousers hold their shape better. For them, it can be worth the extra effort and expense in alteration fees to have trousers lined at the store. (Manufacturers almost never line trousers.) I am not in favor of lining trousers. Unless expertly chosen and sewn, the lining fabric may shrink slightly after cleaning. Then it will cause trousers to hang unevenly. In cold weather, silky lining fabric can feel very cold against bare legs; in hot weather, lined trousers are just that much hotter. If trousers are to be lined, I think a half-lining—from the waist to the knee—is best.

Styling Details

After using your eyes and hands to examine the suit inside out, use clothes sense to judge the outer suit. Consider style points.

Lapel width. The width of lapels on the jacket depends on your taste, but a suit for the world of business (or anywhere else) never has lapels that touch a man's arms. No matter what his build, every man looks broad-chested and well-heeled with a simple notched lapel about three to four inches wide. In the last decade, lapels grew increasingly wide, until they almost touched the shoulders. Now the style is beginning to shift back to narrower lapels; I like slightly narrower lapels in the suits I design, because they help create a long, lean look.

Pockets. There are two varieties of pockets: patch, in which the entire pocket is applied to the outer surface like a patch; and inset (also called set-in), hidden except for the pocket opening. Patch pockets belong on casual clothes, such as tweed suits or blazers. More formal suits should always have inset pockets. The small ticket pocket sometimes found just above one hip pocket is always an inset (but it's seen less commonly now).

Flaps on pockets have one practical advantage. Suits of the man who often stuffs his hands into the jacket pockets eventually display pocket sag. This gaping doesn't show under a flap. On the

In selecting styling details, consider width of lapels, decoration in pocket or buttonhole, pocket style, number of vents, and type of trouser bottom.

other hand, there is a small visual advantage to the unflapped inset pocket. It creates a more narrow-hipped look. It's no big deal, but if heft is your problem, you might consider unflapped pockets.

Breast pocket and buttonhole in the lapel are usually best left alone. If you like the idea, you can stick a handkerchief into the breast pocket. No elaborate folds or fancy points, though. Just tuck it in. Some fashionable men of Group C and Group D enjoy wearing a fresh flower in the buttonhole. If it pleases you, why not? But never both flower and pocket handkerchief together. One clean touch of color can make a man look dapper. Two look spotty and fussy.

Suit backs. These should be as plain, simple, and clean-lined as possible. Your suit should suggest powerful shoulders and a long, strong spine. Tacked-on belts, accordion pleats, bellows backs, and other gimmicks work against that ideal.

Vents are the only legitimate detail for the suit back. But not even the vent is strictly necessary, and there is a current tendency in Europe to do away with vents in the interest of a slimmer look to the torso. Side vents are the most desirable for a man who has the habit of putting his hands into his trouser pockets. They will help him look neater from the rear view. Side vents also for the fellow who has a big rear end. Even when the jacket fits well, a center vent sometimes parts unattractively over an ample seat. Otherwise, no vent or a center vent provides a longer, somewhat more elegant line.

Cuffs. Reserve cuffs for the trousers of suits that could conceivably be worn in the country (a tweed suit, plain medium gray flannel, tan poplin, etc.). Suits that look good for formal business and evening wear (navy blue serge, dark gray flannel, dark blue- or gray-and-white pinstripes, etc.) should never have cuffed trousers. Cuffs are still called "turn-ups" in England. Originally they were a do-it-yourself device for clothes care. A man turned up the bottoms of his pants before setting out on a country walk to guard them from mud, dust, dung, and burrs. In town, even before paved streets, this was unnecessary because a gentleman went about in a carriage. None of us today would refer to himself as a "gentleman" any more than his wife would call herself a "lady." Yet cuffs still are considered inappropriate for gentlemanly "town" clothes. Cuffs also break the visual line of a long leg. Few men need that, whether in or out of town.

Trouser width. The width of trouser legs varies with current style waves, but pants for a business suit should never be as skinny as jeans or as wide as skirts. I would advise no narrower than 19 inches at the knee for suit pants. If thighs are heavy, 19½ inches. Width at the bottom would then be 19 to 20 inches. If you wear a somewhat higher heel, even 21 inches at the bottom is good to provide the proper drape over the instep. Wider than 21 inches, the trousers start looking like Charlie Chaplin's.

Trouser length. The length of trousers is much more important than many men seem to realize. *The single greatest clothing mistake the average American man makes is wearing his pants too short.* A well-dressed man should never have his socks showing unless he's seated. As a very general rule, trousers should fall straight down to the shoe and cover about half the shoe in front. In back, they should slope, or cant, down to hang one-quarter inch or even one-half inch lower over the back of the shoe. That is for uncuffed trousers. Trousers with cuffs hang perfectly straight in front and behind. But again, they must be long enough to cover about half the shoe. Always watch this detail carefully.

About Vests

Unless you always wear your jacket in the office (and I can think of hardly anybody who does), a vest is usually helpful for maintaining a power image in the world of business. It always looks more pulled-together than shirt and pants alone, with or without a tie, and it offers handy pockets for impedimenta. The vest has a royal history: Samuel Pepys credits Charles II with the invention, in 1666, of the vest. The correct way of wearing a vest today has another connection with British royalty. George IV, when Prince

Regent in the early nineteenth century, forgot to button the last button of his vest before a party. The loyal Beau Brummel, seeing the ruler's lapse, immediately unbuttoned the lowest button of his own vest, and the fashion was set. It's still the way to wear a vest today. The other way is close-fitting. It should fit like a second skin.

The vest can match the trousers or not. In casual-dress businesses, it can be brown suede or whatever. It may even be a sleeveless V-neck sweater that adds the trim note when working without a jacket, but this is looked upon as very informal for most office situations and, except for a cardigan, doesn't usually offer the convenience of pockets. You look taller and invariably more "dressed" in a vest that matches your trousers.

Protecting Your Investment in Suits and Jackets

· Always use a shaped wooden or plastic hanger, not the skinny wire kind from the dry cleaner, to store your suit jacket and vest. If you can possibly afford the closet space, hang trousers separately on wooden clamp bar hangers. Wrinkles and creases will fall out through the weight of the pants. They should be the kind of trouser hangers that open at the hook and clamp shut. Don't use the kind with clamps at either end, as they can leave "tooth marks" in your trousers.

· Slick finish hangers are better than raw wood ones. A rough hanger can damage the lining of a suit. Run your hand over the top of the hangers when you buy them. If they feel splintery to your palm, pass them by.

· Throw out the metal hanger when a suit comes back from the cleaner. But keep the clear plastic bag and the tissue paper overlay on the shoulders. Unless you store suits in individual garment bags, it's the best way of keeping them in perfect condition. If a new suit comes with a zip-up vinyl garment bag, keep it, and keep the suit in it. But leave the bag unzipped to let air circulate. Your suit will maintain its looks longer.

· Suits worn in the rain or on hot, humid days, should be dried thoroughly (on the right kind of hanger and with plenty of circulating air) before being taken in for pressing.

· At the start of cooler weather, take heavier suits out of the garment bag in which they have been stored for summer and hang them in the bathroom before wearing. Hang suits from the shower curtain bar, draw a hot bath, and close the door to "steam" your suits. After half an hour, give each suit a light, brisk brushing and it will look fresh from the cleaner's.

· Velvet suits and jackets are best revived by brushing first, then steaming.

5

Shirt Power

When others look at you, they notice your face first. Use the shirt you wear to influence what they see there.

When you don't look or feel up to par, don't wear a crisp white broadcloth shirt. White, especially in such a high-reflecting smooth finish, will act like a spotlight, throwing a harsh glare up onto a drawn, pallid face. If company policy demands white, then make it soft and low-reflecting oxford cloth. Otherwise, wear a soft blue oxford cloth. The color contrast makes skin look healthier. A button-down collar offers a small distraction for the eye and focuses it away from the face. Use the tie you wear for more image-manipulation. Matte textures—wool knit or wool challis, cotton madras—flatter a fatigued face to make it seem shinier through contrast. Gleaming silk does not. Tie color could be anything fairly muted and with enough pattern to distract; small-scale plaids, paisleys or geometrics in soft reds or quiet blues are best.

When in peak form, call attention to the fact with a crisp white shirt. Always wear white shirts at night to avoid being lost in the shadows. At night, white lights up the face and looks fresh and clean as no other color can.

But selecting shirts for flattery isn't the major consideration. Let's take the points of a business shirt one by one.

Ready-made vs. Custom

Practically every man can be well dressed with good ready-mades. If it fits correctly (I'll get to that in a minute), buy it. You'll save time and money. You will spend somewhere between $15 and $30 for the shirt and can wear it right away.

At a custom shirtmaker, you decide on cloth and style after a series of detailed measurements is taken. Then you wait—several weeks, depending on the workroom—before going back for a fitting. Then wait again until the shirt is ready, perhaps two months from the day you placed your order. The average tab for a custom-made shirt is upward of $50. Unless you have a truly abnormal build or just more time and money than you know what to do with, I don't see the point.

A compromise is effected in some men's stores. Semicustom or a similar term is used for this. A selection of cloths, collars, and cuffs is available. You choose from these and have measurements taken. You place your order—usually for a stipulated minimum of four to six shirts—then wait. Four to six weeks later (no fittings) the shirts are ready at a cost of $25 to $50 or so, depending on the fabric you select. The shirts are sure to fit you well. But if a slip-up in the order has taken place, or you don't care for the look of the finished shirt, you may have big problems in not accepting it.

For time, money, and prepurchase assurance that you will like the shirt, I say it's ready-made hands down. But get it to fit.

The Way Shirts Should Fit

Ask to be measured any time you buy a shirt. It's the only way to be sure you are buying the size that's right for you right now. Take up a new sport, go back to the gym, lay off the booze, stop smoking, or watch your weight for one month and you will probably slightly change the collar size and sleeve length you need in

The way a shirt fits: (a) collar fits closely, with just enough room to insert little finger; (b) cuffs fit closely and show from one-half to three-quarters of an inch below jacket sleeve; (c) tapered shirts give neater appearance than box-cut shirts.

a shirt. Arms don't lengthen with exercise, but the back becomes more muscular. That affects sleeve length, since the measurement is taken from the middle of the back down to the wristbone. Always ask to be measured before looking over the shirts available in what you think is your size.

Cuffs. Shirt cuffs should come to a point just below the wristbone. They should be long enough to show from one-half to three-quarters of an inch below the jacket sleeve. I like three-quarters of an inch of shirt cuff to show. Men of Group A or Group B may consider that too flashy or dramatic. But every man should show at least one-half inch of cuff. Less suggests you borrowed the shirt or just don't know or care about clothes.

Cuffs should fit closely. Too loose ones have a way of riding up into the jacket sleeve.

French cuffs or button cuffs are personal style decisions. French cuffs do look very elegant, though. Barrel cuffs with two attached buttons, rather than one, are as trim and formal as French cuffs and less trouble.

Collar. Cary Grant often wears shirt collars a fraction larger than perfect fit would demand. He hasn't explained why, but perhaps it's because a collar that is very slightly loose subtly prevents a muscular neck from appearing too thick. If a man is putting on weight, the slightly loose collar may suggest that he is losing weight instead.

Playing around with details of fit in that way can be effective. It is also very tricky. Unless you are sure of the result, have your shirt collar fit closely enough so you can just slide your little finger into the space between collar and neck.

The height and spread of the collar are always relative to the length of a man's neck and the shape of his face.

If your neck is very short, the collar should slope down to be no more than one inch above the collarbone. Use your thumb as a handy rule. With thumbnail against your neck and side of the thumb resting on the collarbone, the top of the thumb should hit just about where your collar should. Most men with short necks find a narrow spread and moderately long points provide the best collar style.

With a long neck and thin face, you will want a higher collar, perhaps up to three inches above the collarbone. A moderate spread and points that are not too long will make your face look broader. You may, however, prefer the opposite effect. A friend of mine, John Galliher, is very much a Group C man—elegant, witty, impeccable—with a lean, aristocratic face. His shirts always have a moderately high collar but with collar points that are wide and flared. This makes his face seem leaner, more aristocratic than ever.

A wide spread on a low collar can make a wide face appear stronger and will emphasize a strong jaw. Older men sometimes find it advantageous to wear higher collars, even if their necks are not especially long, to cover wrinkles.

The best collar for you can only be arrived at by individual consideration. You don't want to buy a lot of experimental shirts. There is a way to determine the best collar style free of charge, though.

Check out the selection of collar shapes in the semicustom department of a good men's store. Then ask to see a ready-made shirt with a collar like the one that seems right. Or look over a variety of ready-mades that are all in the same color. Looking at several white shirts together makes style points more apparent than if you are trying to spot the differences in detail while trying to ignore color and pattern which will influence and confuse judgment of what's best and most appealing.

When you find a collar shape that's right, stick with it. I don't mean you should always wear exactly the same thing. But if you need a high collar, look for that. You'll find it. Remember the name of the manufacturer who made a shirt with the right collar for you. Chances are good that, whether plain point or button-down, other shirts of that make will work well for you.

Body. The shirt body should be long enough not to pull out of the trousers when you move, and just wide enough to give an inch or so of play. Tapered shirts are always neater looking than box-cut ones, and any man who keeps himself in trim should consider them. Women seem to prefer the neater look of tapered shirts on any man who doesn't have a bulging middle. Many people I know who like the fabrics and styles of shirts from Brooks Brothers, but not the very wide cut, buy there and then take the shirts in to a cleaner who does alterations and shirt repairs to have the slack taken out of the middle.

Shirting Fabrics

For comfort, looks, and "hand," cotton is the ideal fabric for business shirts. It always looks rich and cool, and it grows softer with each washing and ironing. For many men—and their wives—that's the hassle about cotton. Ironing. I have heard people in stores insist on permanent-press shirts because they can be machine-washed and worn without pressing. Maybe. But after a few washings those shirts definitely need some kind of touch-up ironing or they look less than perfect. That might be all right for some situations, but appearances count too much in the world of business to wear a so-so shirt. I always feel better starting out the day in a fresh, crisp, professionally ironed cotton shirt. Of course, I don't expect others to iron my shirts unless they're paid to do it. Ironing is no fun. But having shirts professionally laundered is not such a big expense. You won't be able to deduct cleaning costs from your income tax as a business expenditure, but you should look at it as such. It's a small price to pay for looking your best.

There may be another consideration: the crispness of synthetics. I don't deny that cotton "wilts" after a long, hot day. If you require a really unrumpled look, there are some excellent polyester-and-cotton blends. But look for the blend that has the highest percentage of cotton, say no lower than 60 percent, if you want the best look and feel.

Shirts that are made completely of man-made fibers are a bad idea for the world of business. Most of them look shiny and synthetic. When they don't, they still tend to be a little clammy to the touch; and they can be very hot to wear, since they don't absorb moisture or help it to evaporate. And if you perspire in an acrylic or nylon shirt, you'd better wash it right away and fast. Otherwise, it acquires and keeps a peculiar smell.

Silk offers top-of-the-line luxury in shirt fabrics, but it looks a little too rich and formal for wear with most daytime business suits.

Color and Pattern in Business Shirts

The lightest, softest colors you can find—ivory, ecru, pale blue, palest pink, pale clear yellow, and white—look richest and are most flattering for shirts in solid colors. Stay away from any dark solid shirt for business, unless you work for a godfather. Because so many people dislike them and so few people look good in them anyway, you should also avoid solid-color business shirts in brown, navy, green, lavender, purple, red, or orange. They look cheap.

Patterns offer more leeway in color for business shirts, as do patterned fabrics for business suits. Still, to make coordination easier, it is wise to stay away from green, lavender, purple, and orange in shirts as well as suits when choosing patterns.

Any pale color you would use for a solid shirt looks good in a patterned one. In addition, brown, dark blue, wine red, dark gray, and even black can be appropriate and handsome for patterned business shirts—as long as they are on a white or very pale ground. In the most casual kind of business situation, a dark tartan plaid might be attractive; but as a general rule, you should save plaids for after hours.

The kind of pattern you wear for the world of business is very important. The operative words are: discreet, soft-focus, low-key. Remember, too, pattern of any kind is considered less formal than a solid color. Among more conservative members of the international power elite, solid-color pale blue or ivory shirts are the most acceptable for business wear before six, solid white the only acceptable shirt after six.

While you must consider your audience, most of us enjoy the variety of pattern in business shirts, and the liveliness can be used to good advantage by every man. So that the pattern doesn't

upstage you or undercut your image of competence, avoid those that are overbearing.

Look for something fine-lined. Pinstripes are the width of a straight pin, up to one-sixteenth of an inch wide. You can't go wrong with them. Thin stripes that are wider-spaced are excellent too. Keep in mind, though, the wider the stripe, the softer the color should be. Heavy and wide stripes of charcoal gray on white are unflattering and unbusinesslike. Candy stripes, about one-eighth of an inch wide, are the widest I would recommend for a two-color stripe.

Thick-and-thin stripes often look very luxurious and have interesting colorations. They are usually seen in more expensive shirtings, and they look it. But it's wise to stick to no more than two colors plus white for shirts you wear for business. When there are more than three colors in a shirt, it should be saved for nonbusiness hours.

Very neat, delicate windowpane and tattersall checks as well as miniature gingham checks are other pattern possibilities for your business shirts. They should meet the same requirements as striped shirts: overall impression of pale color, and no more than two colors plus white per shirt. In addition, you should recognize that checked or plaid shirts are always a less formal choice than stripes.

You might occasionally find some other pattern that you recognize as right for business shirts—as Serge Obolensky found the pinhead dots I mentioned before but I doubt it.

Since patterns tend to be more restricted in their use, I advise you to concentrate on building a broad stock of solid-color shirts first, just as in acquiring business suits you lay in the blue chips before venturing into glamour stocks. Security, not monotony, is the idea.

You may be surprised to discover the difference texture makes. Take as an example the pale blue shirt. In broadcloth, it is silky and rather formal; in oxford cloth, softer and more casual. Somewhere between the two in texture and degree of formality there is end-on-end madras. Pale blue chambray is less formal than any of them, very different in texture, but still the same pale color.

Add satin-stripe voile or jacquard-weave cotton with a raised pattern, and you have half a dozen pale blue shirts—alike in color, but totally different in effect and all totally correct for business wear. Consider the enormous variety within solid colors before you invest in patterned shirts that may be locked into wear with only one or two suits.

Details on Business Shirts

The fewer details the better. Epaulets should be saved for after hours. You may find a breast pocket on your shirt handy, but pockets on both sides make the shirt look too sporty for business wear. Nobody will shoot you for having pockets on the shirt you wear for business—it's just that you don't need them. To look well-dressed in the world of business, you will probably wear a suit jacket. If you take it off in the office, you may still be wearing a vest. What, then, is the need for a pocket in your shirt?

Monograms are a small but telling detail often added to custom or semicustom shirts. If you like them, you can surely find someone to add monograms to your ready-made shirts too. Most discreet and elegant placement for a shirt monogram is that point below the breast and about three inches above the belt on the left side. Embroidery can be any color. Thread that matches the color of the shirt or repeats one color of the shirting pattern is always the most refined choice. If you want fire-engine red, have it, but keep it small and discreet. A monogram should always be done in straightforward style using block letters no more than one-quarter of an inch high. Stay away from lozenges and diamonds that contain odd-shaped letters.

How Many Shirts?

No matter what doesn't come back from the laundry on time, you will be well supplied with business shirts if you have four that work with each suit. Having any fewer demands more careful organization as well as more frequent replacements, because every shirt must be worn and laundered often. When I say shirts that work with each suit, I don't mean just color and pattern. Often I have found that a shirt collar was the wrong shape—a little too spread or too narrow—to look right with a suit, especially if suit and shirt were bought at different times. When buying your suit, always get a couple of shirts that go well with it. Get them in the same store and assemble the whole combination then and there.

Protecting Your Investment in Shirts

· Marks from ballpoint pens can be removed from a shirt if you spray the ink stain with hair spray and then launder as usual. The spray first dissolves the ink and looks as if it's only spreading the stain, but it all comes out in the wash. For pencil marks, use a clean rubber eraser before washing.

· If white buttons on a shirt come back yellowed from the laundry, try rubbing with an ink eraser to clean them.

· If you find a wrinkled shirt collar when you unpack while traveling, you can do a pretty fair ironing job by rubbing it over a hot light bulb. You can also coax out wrinkles overnight by sprinkling a little water on the collar and pressing it flat against a mirror or bathtub.

· Starch makes ironing easier, which is why laundries like it. It also shortens the life of a shirt, so request no starch. If you like the crispness of a starched shirt, ask to have the starch left out of collar and cuffs.

· If you are caught without collar stays of the right length for the shirt you will wear, make your own. Cut them to fit from a shirt cardboard or a plastic wallet-size calendar from the bank; or bend them to fit from large paper clips or pipe cleaners.

· Soak a perspiration-stained shirt in cold, very salty water before laundering it, and you'll remove every trace of the stain.

· Let a wet or damp shirt dry before throwing it into the hamper, especially in summer or in humid climates. Stains can become fixed otherwise, and you may even find the shirt mildewed.

· Always check to be sure you have removed collar stays before sending shirts out to the laundry. It's easy to forget this, and if you do, the stays can melt into the fabric during pressing.

6

The Necktie: Nonverbal Advertising

How to Select a Tie

Neckties communicate your attitude and your position immediately and prominently. Choose them with the same consideration you would devote to selecting a business letterhead or a spot ad on TV.

You have discarded by now those ties that failed the times-worn test. If not, get rid of them now. The "perfectly good" tie that looks to you like a near-miss, the ones you feel you could wear but somehow never do, will downgrade the look of everything else you wear.

Perhaps it's time for a few new ones. The average American man buys twelve ties each year. Since the ties you want for the power look will probably cost between $10 and $25 each, that's over $150 a year in outlay. But there's a lot of potential business and social return riding on it. Buy carefully to get maximum pleasure and profit.

There are five points to consider in ties.

Length. When knotted, the tie should meet, but not overlap, your belt buckle. The tip should be just where your navel is. Good ties have a standard length of approximately fifty-seven inches. That works for men with neck sizes of up to seventeen inches. Whether that's the right length for you depends on how you tie it. The Windsor knot uses up the greatest amount of tie length; four-in-hand, the least. If you are high-waisted or short, try out the Windsor knot. The four-in-hand will probably be most satisfactory for someone tall and thin. Just make sure the tie touches the top of the pants.

Width. The width of a tie should always be in accord with width of jacket lapels. In the fifties and early sixties, suit lapels were very narrow and ties were only a couple of inches wide. By the early seventies, lapels almost touched the shoulders and ties were almost as wide as mufflers. Now, the trend is back to narrower ties; three to four inches is the right width. The measurement is taken at the blade (or widest point) of the tie. About three to four inches is the going width for lapels, too. The measurement— and the wave of style—will probably change someday. When it does, don't fight it, but don't immediately rush out and buy several new ties that don't work with your old suits. It's much better, for the world of business especially, to be too conservative than to be overly experimental or inconsistent.

Noël Coward once told me that, whatever the style of the moment was, a man should wear his ties wider and his hair shorter at the rate of a quarter of an inch per decade. Shorter hair does more to make the face seem open and alert, and the broad knot of a wider tie can help balance downward sag.

Guts. Not yours, but the tie's. Good construction means the tie will knot well, look substantial, and recover its shape between wearings. There should be an interlining of coarse, plain-weave muslin. Ties made of heavy fabrics need a single thickness of interlining, while cotton and light silk take a double thickness. You may not even see the interlining—good ties are often given an interfacing of thin silk which may hide the muslin. Don't tear up a tie to see whether it's lined properly. Turn back the folds inside the blade and you will see the interlining. If not, rub the tie gently between your thumb and forefinger and you can feel it. Perhaps you have heard that the number of dark stripes woven into the muslin interlining is a mark of quality. The truth is, any number of horsehair stripes can be included in lining fabric with no change in cost or quality.

In knit ties, check for a strip of silk sewn on along the narrow part of the tie—where it goes against the inner part of the shirt collar. This prevents friction and lumping when the tie is worn or removed.

The label of the store or manufacturer is often on a strip of fabric that is tacked on to the back of the wide part of the tie. Slide the narrow back part of the tie through this loop, and both parts will stay in place.

Fabric. The four most common fabrics are silk, wool, cotton, and polyester. Silk is the standard luxury material, and a low luster is the standard for good silk. The best polyester is the one that most closely resembles low-luster silk. Polyester usually costs a little less and is sometimes easy to clean. Psychologically, you will feel more affluent and powerful in silk. Spend the extra dollar or two and economize on underwear or socks or something else that's inconspicuous. Don't save money on your ties. It doesn't pay. A good silk tie can be worn at any time of the year. In fall and winter, wool—whether woven or knitted—is handsome, long-wearing, and wrinkle-resistant, and it has a rich look. In hot weather, cotton is the odds-on favorite for most men. The fact that cotton ties wrinkle more easily is compensated for by their low cost and light, cool feeling.

Blends of fibers are found in ties as well as other things you wear. A tie of silk-and-wool, usually called Irish poplin, is excellent. It is crisp, luxurious, and durable. A blend (or synthetic) that has the look of linen is probably a better bet than pure linen. Linen is one of the most easily crushed materials and, in a tie, isn't long-wearing despite its good looks. That's when polyester is a godsend.

Color and Pattern. I saved the biggest points for last, although they are the first things that are usually considered. There can't be any hard-and-fast rules to see you through the choices. But there is one sound guideline to color: the most authoritative effect is achieved when the tie is darker and more intense in color than either suit or shirt.

A deep, rich color always looks expensive. Claret is more elegant than fire-engine red; forest green is more elegant than yellow-green. This does not mean that soft, pale colors are a bad idea. In summer, sky blue neckties can look very good with ecru suits and pale shirts. They look gauche, though, with navy blue suits.

Vivid color in the pattern sparks a dark tie. Even pure white or signal orange in the pattern of a tie can give a needed lift to dark suits. Here is where the most offbeat colors can legitimately come into play for the world of business. But they should be small and restricted to the pattern, not the ground of the tie you wear.

A dime is smaller than a nickel, but worth more. In selecting patterned ties, go for dime-size figures (or smaller) and you can't lose. Among patterns, small polka dots, narrow stripes, repeating geometrics in small scale, miniature plaids, and small paisley designs carry the most clout.

Patterns also have degrees of formality. Small polka dots, very small checks, and narrow stripes are considered the dressiest patterns. Repeating geometrics and paisleys are more informal. Solid-color ties, depending on the material, can go either way. Solid silk twill is formal, solid wool knit informal, but either can move into the opposite category more easily than a patterned tie. As a general rule, the fewer the colors, the more formal the tie. Tiny white dots on blue give you a super-correct formal tie. Multicolor dots, no matter how small, make it a more informal tie.

Which Tie with What?

In coordinating ties with suits and shirts, think of texture before considering color. Your tie is the smallest element in a business turnout. You know it can be the strongest color. It should also have the most pronounced texture: either much smoother or much rougher than the shirt and suit. For example, a tweed suit, oxford cloth shirt, and wool knit tie all share a certain rough, informal texture. The shirt is the least rough of the three, the jacket is rougher, and the tie is the roughest. Conversely, a gabardine suit, broadcloth shirt, and silk foulard tie are all smooth, urbane textures. The silk tie, though, is the element in which this lustrous texture is most evident.

Aside from being texturally more pronounced than the other elements, the tie should also carry the strongest color message, as I said. Don't be overly concerned, though, with matching shades of color. It is very tricky to team, say, tan suit–ecru shirt–brown tie. When this combination is just slightly off, it's awful. Attractive coordination almost invariably results, however, when two (or even all three) of the basic colors of business—tan, navy, gray— are combined. Especially if white or maroon is added. For example: tan suit, gray-and-white striped shirt, slate blue tie. Or navy suit, cream-color shirt, maroon tie. Or gray suit, blue shirt, blue-and-white tie.

How Many Ties?

Two or three ties per suit should see you through. If you wish to cut down on the number, rely heavily on solid-color ties. They are the most versatile.

If there were a fire in my apartment and I set out to replace everything, I would buy just six neckties at first. And four of them would be in solid colors. I would get, as the bare minimum to go with everything:

1 dark blue silk
1 maroon silk
1 dark blue wool knit
1 maroon wool knit
1 crimson-navy-and-white stripe rep silk
1 navy-and-white small polka dot print silk

Protecting Your Investment in Ties

· Give every tie—even your favorite—a rest between wearings. It will hold its shape and look better. Never wear the same tie for two days running.

· When you take off your tie, give it a shake to help release wrinkles from knotting, and then hang it up.

· If you take a steamy shower after undressing, hanging your tie in the bathroom will make it look even better. The moisture and warmth are almost as good as a pressing.

· Knit ties will sag if hung on a tie bar. Try rolling them up and parking them on a shelf between wearings.

· If your tie is badly wrinkled and needs an emergency pressing, do it this way: Cut out a piece of shirt cardboard to fit, and slide it under the face of the tie. This will stop marks from the back side of the tie from showing up on the front. Press lightly and quickly with the iron, using a soft cloth between tie and iron to prevent shine or scorch on the tie.

· Break yourself of the habit (if you have it) of slipping the knot of a tie. Wearing a tie at half-mast with an open collar cuts its life.

· Never remove your tie by slipping the knot and sliding it over your head. Many people do this and even leave the knot formed when they put the tie away. Untie it and hang it or roll it if you want the tie to look good next time it's worn.

· Another habit to break: that of touching your tie at the knot to make sure it's in place. Even if your hands are clean, the tie will eventually look dirty at the throat.

· Despite clean, careful living, ties can get splotched and soiled. When perspiration stains show at the knot, let the stain dry, and then blot the tie with a sponge and cold water. Water spots afflict silk ties. Let them dry, use the back (narrow) part of the tie to give a quick, light rub to the spotted areas. Spills, whether wine, gravy, or ketchup, should be blotted immediately. Blot, don't rub, or you risk imbedding the liquid deep into the weave. Later, you can try holding the tie over a pan of boiling water for a minute, then rubbing with a soft, clean cloth.

The above tips will usually work, but when the spot is major or stubborn, the place is Tie Crafters in New York. You don't have to go there; just drop the tie in an envelope and mail it to them at 116 East 27th Street, New York, N.Y. 10008. For about $2, they do a perfect, professional job of cleaning and restoring your tie. It's mailed back in perfect condition. The local dry cleaner cannot do the same job as this specialist. They handle about eight hundred ties a week and have been doing work on ties alone since 1951.

7

The Props of Power

While appropriate suits, shirts, and ties are crucial to the power look in business, auxiliary clothing is also important. Apparently small details such as the color of socks and gloves or the type of brief-case carried can enhance or detract from an otherwise crisp, professional appearance. Here we'll look at some of the accessories that work best to reinforce the suits, shirts, and ties that are right for you.

On Top of Everything Else: Coats for Business Wear

For practical purposes, the only coat most men need for business is a tan raincoat with a detachable liner for warmth. The best looking and most versatile is the classic trenchcoat model in khaki. "Trenchcoat," because it was first worn in the trenches during World War I by British officers. Half a million coats during that war, and more than a million trenchcoats since, have been made by the originator, Burberry's. Every manufacturer of rainwear now makes a version of the trenchcoat. It is flattering to almost every man, whether it is worn with belt cinched or loose, coat buttoned or not. Do stick with the original tan color; it's the classic for raincoats, and it has the widest acceptance. As black leather jackets and black gloves have a negative connotation for many people, so do black or dark-color raincoats. Perhaps it's because they suggest underworld villains skulking in the shadows. Better to look like a CIA spy or a Humphrey Bogart detective. The tan raincoat can be worn anywhere, anytime. It's always right in the business world. It looks fine for all leisure wear too, over black tie and dinner suit, or with jeans and a sweater.

For the fun of wearing something different, and for packing a little more individual style into their turnouts, most men who live in colder climates prefer to have another coat or two for business in addition to the raincoat. If you feel this way, get the richest-looking coat you can afford. The top-of-the-line models are the navy blue cashmere coat with plain lines and fly front and the camel's hair polo coat.

A good coat will be serviceable for many, many years since it really gets much less wear, even in Minneapolis or Montreal, than the average suit. For that reason, choose the very simplest and most classic lines when buying a coat for business wear. Exaggerated effects that are fashionable right now may be long forgotten before the coat wears out.

A couple of years ago, a young friend just out of law school and about to start as an associate in a New York law firm was shopping for a warm overcoat. His choice was between two camel's hair coats, both of which looked handsome on him. The first was below-the-knee length, with wide flared lapels and a tie belt. In it he looked modern, stylish, dashing. The second was a standard polo coat—length just above the knee, double-breasted, traditionally cut. In it he looked businesslike, sober, elegantly well dressed. The traditional polo coat felt more "me," he said, but he was also attracted to the stylish reflection of himself in the first model. He was about to toss a coin to decide which to get when the salesman asked him what he did. Lawyer, he said. The salesman then advised him to buy the polo coat. He did and was immediately glad about his choice, and still is. Perhaps the other would have been all right if he'd been in another business—clothing designer or record producer, maybe—but for a lawyer or banker it was inappropriate for everyday wear to work.

Unless you can afford to replace clothes frequently, stick to classic lines for coats worn to the office.

Shoe Power

In his book *Power,* Michael Korda wrote: "The right shoes won't *make* you powerful, but . . . in learning to read the symbols of power . . . shoes are basic."

The power look begins with a suit. It culminates in the perfect shoe, perfectly cared for. For me, it was best expressed by the most astute shaper of international style, Diana Vreeland: "A run-down shoe is the end of civilization."

Always and everywhere, men who care for the opinion of others care for their shoes conscientiously. For some aristocratic Spanish men this includes polishing the sole of the shoe for the same clean gleam as the upper. The English are remarkably consistent about inserting shoe trees immediately after removing their shoes. As a result, even the oldest shoe worn by an Englishman has a sole that fits the floor as neatly as the upper fits the foot. Turned-up toes are as sloppy as scuffed shoes in the iconography of power. The man who communicates power cleans and polishes his shoes before each wearing. A dirty shoe is never powerful as a symbol; it suggests lack of organization.

In the past, shoes could be classified as "walking" or "sitting" ones. The truly elegant shoe was so thin in the sole and so snug on the foot as to make walking almost impossible; the walking shoe was too clumsy for indoor wear. Insistence on mobility has made the sitting shoe obsolete. The cult of the practical walking shoe resulted in the thick, storm-welted brogue, heavy as a dumbbell, worn almost continually a few years back as a weighty badge of respectable masculinity. The best shoes now are neither delicate and constricting nor heavy and cumbersome. Today we recognize the well-made lightweight shoe as symbolic of both sanity and masculine style.

The most useful and elegant shoe for business is simple—no tricky combination of leather and cloth, no confetti coloring. It is a shoe that fits the foot comfortably, that merits attention but does not cry out to be noticed.

Rich dark brown, mahogany, and black are the shoe colors preferred by men of power for the world of business. Authoritative suits are better balanced by these dark colors than by pale ones. The color order of nature—earth and darker colors below, lighter sky above—suggests one reason for this system of visual harmony. The idiomatic contrast between being "light-footed" and having "both feet on the ground" supplies another. But whatever its color, the power shoe is always the clean, simple one. The best quality leather looks handsomest and lasts longest.

WHICH SHOE AND WHEN?

It's no secret that a man who knows he is dressed appropriately has a better time than one who's worried about his attire. Whether at a party or in a duck blind, he is more comfortable physically and mentally. Yet men lag far behind women in recognizing that no one style of shoe, no matter how comfortable, will make us comfortable in all situations.

People noticed the incongruity of Richard Nixon's polished black business shoes and his sporty open shirt and slacks in that famous photo of him walking on the beach. Many of the same people see nothing funny about wearing black wingtips with a dinner jacket. They should.

Categories—business, casual, and dress—blur and overlap to a certain degree now, but there are a few perennial guidelines for looking authentic in the world of business.

You don't *have* to wear lace-up shoes. Some men—usually older—feel that without shoestrings, it's unfit for the office. Younger members of the power elite recognize that slip-on shoes can offer the same substantial construction, fit, and good looks in a less troublesome form. Coming up is a whole generation to whom shoestrings are unknown outside of track or tennis shoes.

But, for the foreseeable future, lace-up shoes will retain a powerful aura in the business world. Consider them first when weighing your options.

LACE-UP SHOES FOR THE WORLD OF BUSINESS

Oxford is the name to remember. You will also run across the terms *blucher* and *brogue*. Ignore them. They are clunky shoes. The blucher is made with vamp and tongue in one piece. The quarters extend to the vamp and overlap the tongue. Cordovan bluchers were popular for business wear twenty years ago. More than a hundred years before, the shoe was named for the commander of the Prussian forces at Waterloo, Field Marshal von Blücher, and it still suggests a *lumpen* foot soldier who is out of place in a boardroom. *Brogue* meant "shoe" in the old Irish language. The *brocs* of the peat bogs were heavy and heelless untanned leather. Current brogues are heavy and still look better suited to bog-trotting than to policy-making situations. Stick to oxfords.

You will find three varieties. The wingtip oxford is a classic for the world of business, but a limited-use classic. It's great with a dark business suit, but too formal and busy in design for tweeds or more informal suits. The perforated trim looks too utilitarian to be desirable with a dinner jacket. The straight-tip oxford (also known as cap-toe oxford) is a more formal business shoe than the wingtip. It has a thin, straight seam across the toe. Most formal, yet most useful because of its versatility, is the plain-toe oxford. In black, it is correct with business suits in the day or evening and is an ideal choice with a dinner jacket; hence, it can be considered the one lace-up style every man should own.

SLIP-ON SHOES FOR THE WORLD OF BUSINESS

There is a slip-on shoe to meet every requirement, from most formal to least. But the same slip-on doesn't meet all trains.

Every man can use some form of loafer. The original is the penny loafer. Without pennies, this is a standby for many important men. Alexander Liberman, not only a major artist who is represented in such museums as the National Gallery in Washington and the Museum of Modern Art in New York, but

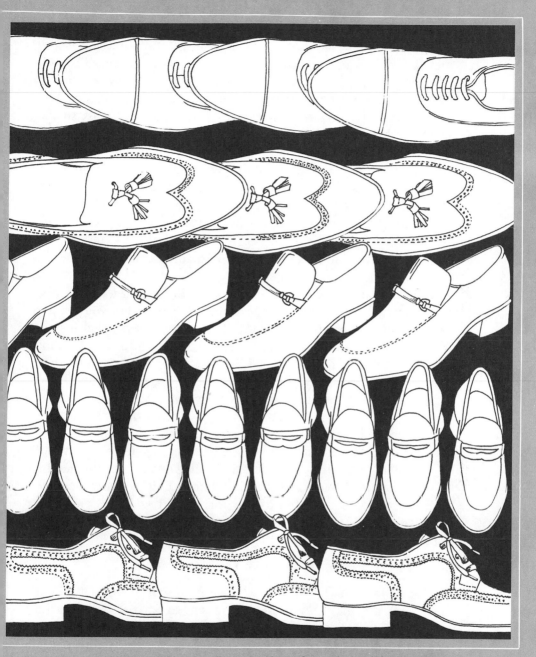

Shoes for the World of Business (from the top): *straight-tip or cap-toe oxfords; tassel loafers; Gucci loafers; penny loafers; wing-tip oxfords.*

also editorial director of the prestigious Condé Nast Publications (*Vogue, Glamour, House & Garden*, etc.), most often wears gleaming black penny loafers with his dark gray custom-tailored suits.

Gucci loafers are a dressier variation. The seam (where vamp and sides are joined) is neatly bound to hide the stitching. The penny slot over the instep is replaced by a glittering brass snaffle bit. Whether from the source or simply a good copy, this style has become a worldwide classic, admired everywhere but not to be worn at all times. It is sporty. It is great with jeans, with informal daytime clothes. It looks good with blazer and slacks for the evening, and is passable with a suit (but a plainer shoe is more appealing than a metal-trimmed one). It is all wrong with black tie. In French, *clinquant* means, roughly, "flashy." Consider the combination of shiny satin on lapels and shiny gold chains on the instep and you get the picture.

Tassel loafers are a refinement of the style, usually with a more tapered toe. Distinctive features, of course, are the leather tassels (sometimes metal-tipped) that dangle over the instep. William Rossi, former podiatrist and now a consultant to shoe manufacturers, says in his book *The Sex Life of the Foot and Shoe* that throughout history the shoe has been a phallic symbol, and tassels represent testicles. John Molloy, who conducts motivational research on the psychological effects of clothing, says in his book *Dress for Success* that tassel shoes should not be worn when looking for a job. Perhaps the best slip-on for an interview would be one with plain toe and sides, a stitched-down flat ornamentation of matching leather across the instep. This is also a possible alternative to the plain-toe oxford for black tie. The monk-strap shoe is very similar, but a shiny metal buckle makes it undesirable for evening wear.

BOOTS IN THE WORLD OF BUSINESS

Rossi states, in *The Sex Life of the Foot and Shoe*, that a boot on a man who has no professional reason to wear it is "a macho expression." Macho is expressed at work these days not just by booted ranchers but also by men who ride herd on junior execs. Maybe it isn't macho only. As Freud once pointed out, besides being a phallic symbol, a cigar is a cigar.

Boots can rarely be worn with a business suit. But if they are, they must be the most expensive and beautiful boots available—otherwise they look tacky or inappropriate. They must have no "Home on the Range" or storm trooper connotations. If you're in doubt, keep boots for nonbusiness hours. Another vital point: Boots that stand comfortably away from the calf are apt to cause an odd break in the straight hang of trouser legs. That's to be avoided.

HOW MANY?

Ideally, a man never wears the same pair of shoes twice in a week. Ideally, too, he wears the best shoes he can afford, so the expense could be major unless he cares for his shoes well. Within reason, though, you need have only two good pairs of black shoes and a pair of brown shoes. For the world of business, you might even plan your wardrobe so as to eliminate the need for brown shoes. With two good pairs of black shoes, you need never wear the same ones two consecutive days, although the blue suit on Monday and the gray on Tuesday both call for black shoes. After a day's wear, shoes need one or preferably two days (with trees inserted) of rest. Otherwise they will wear out (and get smelly) sooner. After wear in the rain, two days is the minimum for proper drying that is essential to long life for the shoe and proper health for the foot. Always wear a pair of galoshes in the rain or snow, or else shoes will get totally ruined.

If finances permit, you should also have the brown shoes for the world of business. They are a good choice with all suit colors, even navy blue in the right circumstances. But, to the power elite, there is something unappealing about a man who wears brown shoes after dark, so if you are economizing on your shoe invest-ment, stick to black.

BLUE-CHIP INVESTMENTS IN BUSINESS SHOES

Whatever his power style grouping, a man is well shod with:

1 pair black plain-toe oxfords
1 pair black plain-toe slip-ons
1 pair black (or brown) loafers, metal or leather trim

Add as many more to this list as your needs demand, but get these first and get the best. Bear in mind that the condition of your feet determines not only your success in achieving the power look but also the health and energy of your entire body.

Socks

For the business world socks are of one model (over the calf) and one color range (dark). Best materials are thin wool, cotton lisle, and blends. They should never be very sheer or very heavy. Don't match your socks to the suit you wear or to the shoes. Their color should always relate to the color of your tie. Not match it, but relate to it. If the tie is red-and-white, the socks to wear are maroon. If it's blue, navy socks, and so on. One exception—although I don't recommend solid white ties, if you wear one, don't wear white socks with it. Gray or black socks are better.

Wallet

Some men carry with them as many as fifty credit and I.D. cards, most of which overlap or duplicate in function. Rather than using a wallet with bulky, accordion-fold housing for cards you don't need to carry with you, use a slim billfold and safely store most of your cards somewhere else. You should be covered for any situation if you have with you one or two major national credit cards, your driver's license, and perhaps a bank identification card. The thinnest wallet with the fewest contents will make your suit look and fit better.

The color of your wallet doesn't matter as much as its material. It should be fine, supple, polished leather. You can't go wrong with a plain dark maroon, rich brown, or black one. (I particularly like those with simple gold-metal reinforcement on the corners.)

Wearing a breast-pocket wallet for business always suggests greater affluence than keeping a wallet in the pants pocket, probably because men in command have traditionally worn suits, and this is the most convenient place for a wallet when wearing a suit. If you work in shirtsleeves, keep the wallet in your back pocket thin, too. Surprisingly, there's a sound medical reason as well as an aesthetic one: *Vogue* reported that Dr. Nathaniel Gould of Brockton, Massachusetts, was able to trace several cases of painful sciatica that were caused simply by sitting against a lumpy back pocket.

Briefcase

A beautiful attaché case makes a perfect gift for any occasion. A good attaché case is always useful, and carrying one always looks good. Small hand or shoulder bags, often carried by stylish European men, somehow don't. Even on via Condotti, the briefcase has a more masculine look.

The kind to carry is the best you can afford. It's often better to carry nothing, or a manila envelope, while saving for a good leather attaché case than to spoil your look with a really cheesy plastic case. Most men at the very top, who have aides and executive secretaries to tote for them, are seen without an attaché case. I find I prefer the independence of having it all personally in hand. My briefcase is usually loaded with junk. Even when it has no business papers inside, it is convenient for stashing sunglasses, keys, whatever.

Plain dark brown leather is your best bet. Luggage tan is second best. Stay away from gray or black. Avoid fancy hardware and flashy, unusual materials such as ostrich hide and the like. If you are in a more creative profession—advertising, show business, design, etc.—you can get away with a signed designer attaché case if you like. The best are Fendi, Gucci, and Louis Vuitton.

Some very junior executives regard a much-battered attaché case as a sign of seniority. Senior executives usually know that a well-cared-for leather case shows a more organized man. Keep your briefcase in peak condition, polishing it (with neutral color) and caring for it as you would the shoes you wear in the world of business.

A slim leather portfolio is the alternative to the attaché case. It may suggest that you don't really have to drag work home. It can never be confused with a salesman's sample case, but rather, perhaps, with a company president's. This, too, should be ultrasimple, of supple dark brown leather with a side zip, and about 12 by 15 inches.

When traveling, you may find a shoulder bag handy. I'll take up considerations for that in Part III.

Jewelry

I've recently begun designing men's jewelry, and I find it's especially fun because it allows most creativity. Jewelry is largely a matter of personal taste, but there are two general guidelines: Keep it simple; and, in the world of business, keep it to a minimum. Often, men at the top wear (or carry) only two items of jewelry for the world of business—a plain gold wedding ring and a plain gold watch.

Your watch certainly doesn't have to be gold. But you do need a watch in order to make the most efficient use of your time. Your own ideas about efficiency must determine the style. Most useful is a watch with legible numbers, a second hand, and no fuss. A plain Timex will do. If you want to spend more money, a beautiful, expensive gold watch will always enhance your look. For me, and for many of my friends, that's supplied by a Rolex "oyster" watch or a Cartier "tank" watch. You might prefer something entirely different. I would suggest, though, that really strange designs, very sporty models, or Mickey Mouse watches are better for after hours than for business.

Bracelets fall into the same category. I know very elegant men who wear simple bracelets for business. They would seem even more elegant, though, without the metal around the wrist. I.D. bracelets with such vital information as name, blood type, next of kin, etc., serve a purpose. But the purpose could be less obtrusively served with a dogtag, like those of the U.S. Army, worn on a gold chain inside the shirt. These can be bought and engraved at a jeweler's. Cartier even sells solid gold dogtags, if you feel uneasy with anything less. But don't risk making others uneasy with a bracelet.

Small gold signet rings worn on the little finger are quite usual and often have strong sentimental value for the wearer. If you don't wear one now, don't go out and buy one. For a man, the wedding ring is the only ring that is always correct.

Cuff links have the greatest style when closest in size to cuff buttons. The smartest ones are those that are flat gold copies of ordinary buttons. Elegant men also often wear flat gold oval shapes, a hinged gold ring that clamps shut, a small gold ball, or a dumb-bell shape. Try to find cuff links that have two matching sides connected by a short post or chain, rather than those with one face and a twist-bar back. The former are more expensive (and look it); but you only need one pair of cuff links. In most cities, stores that sell old gold and antique jewelry sell cuff links very inexpensively, and you can often find "two-faced" gold cuff links for little money.

Gold isn't the only material. Silver can be very beautiful, and so can enamel. Enamel is less versatile, though. Very traditional haberdashers often sell a kind of knot cuff link. It's just a short length of silky elastic cord with a decorative knot at either end. These cuff links are small, discreet, a great favorite with Ivy Leaguers, and very inexpensive—under $5 a pair the last time I looked in J. Press. Avoid wearing any kind of stone, real or fake, in business cuff links.

The pinned collar is back in favor again, and collar pins of gold-tone or silver-tone metal are perfectly acceptable. If you wear a pinned collar frequently, maybe you would prefer real gold; but they are easy to lose, so be sure that you are a well-organized person before springing for precious metals. I feel the same way about those 18-karat-gold collar stays. They are an amusing pres-ent for a man who's hard to find presents for. But wearing them means he has to be extra careful not to send his shirts off to the laundry with the stays still in the collar.

There are other bits of jewelry—lapel pins, tie tacks, etc.—but before adding things to your suit, shirt, and tie for the world of business, always consider the people with whom you will be dealing; too much or too flashy jewelry will put off many men, particularly the more conservative.

You may also carry a certain amount of jewelry with you in the business world: pen or pencil in gold or silver, a money clip, a cigarette lighter (but not a cigarette case—that's an evening power prop), a key ring. For all these, plain silver or gold is best. But don't go into hock buying any of them. Trinkets of this sort are easily mislaid or stolen. You have more important things on your mind during a business day than keeping up with a gold pen or lighter.

Handkerchiefs

For practicality, it's hard to beat Kleenex. But a white linen handkerchief, fresh as the first snow, is a classic power prop. If it is monogrammed, white embroidery looks best. Sometimes, especially when you want a very dapper effect, you might want to tuck a colored or patterned handkerchief in the breast pocket of your jacket. A touch of the right color can pick up a man's look for business. Getting just the right color is important, though. And there is no hard-and-fast rule about it, except that it should relate to tie color. Experiment before wearing the pocket square. It might take more time than you want to spend on a rushed morning to find the "perfect" thing. If you ever have to question whether the touch of color in your pocket looks too tricky or off-color, forget it. Empty pockets are often to be preferred.

There are two ways of wearing a pocket square. Easiest, and I think better, is as follows: Unfold the handkerchief. Hold it in the center and fold it loosely in half. There are thus five points. Now flatten it, and tuck it points-down into the pocket so that roughly one inch of handkerchief shows. The other way is to let the points show. This involves more discretion, I think, to judge the correct amount of handkerchief display. Too little, and the handkerchief looks like a little row of picket fence; too much, and the floppy points call to mind *fin-de-siècle* dandies.

Scarves

Scarves can be a trial for some men and a boon for others. Keep your throat warm with a muffler and you will stay healthier. If you don't like having it around your throat, though, you will pull and tug at it. That destroys the power look. Never wear anything that makes you feel nervous or ill at ease.

The best scarves for business are cashmere or wool in solid tan, gray, navy, or dark maroon. They may have a reverse face of plain or printed silk that looks like a foulard tie pattern. Very long scarves, white scarves, and elaborately fringed scarves are, if you like them, for the private or off-duty sector, but not recommended for the business world.

Hats

Once an indispensable part of a man's equipment for the world of business, hats give a very distinguished look to those men (usually older and quite conservative) who still wear them. If you feel a hat could be a good addition to your statement of the power look, wear one. But realize that you have to be extra careful of precise dressing and grooming when you wear a hat. For a hat to look dapper rather than foolishly affected, the man under it must be religious about making and keeping appointments with his barber. The business hat he wears should have the smallest brim that balances the width of his face, and the lowest crown that accords with the length of his face and neck. One of the elder statesmen in a good men's store is the salesman to see for working out these visuals. Color should be fairly muted, fairly dark.

The only time a hat is absolutely necessary is with a formal mourning suit. In this case, a black top hat is a must.

I wear a hat only in really cold weather. Did you know that you lose up to 50 percent of your body heat on a cold day by going bareheaded? But for a hat to keep you warm, it has to cover the ears, too. I like those fur hats with ear flaps. They are a legitimate, functional addition to any man's winter attire.

Gloves

Gloves have always been a power symbol. Until the nineteenth century, they were the exclusive province of the clergy, the military, and the nobility; the rank and file were prohibited from wearing them. Now every man who lives in a cold climate should have several pairs of gloves. Especially if you are bothered by poor circulation (as I am), good gloves can make the difference between getting things done in winter and barely getting through it.

Dark brown leather gloves with a lining of knitted fabric or fur are the best bet. They can be worn with everything. Even with black shoes and a dark blue or gray coat, well-dressed men prefer brown gloves to black. Second choice would be gray suede gloves. Third, beige or gray gloves of knitted cashmere or wool. Never black gloves. There seems to be no logical reason that I can discover, but black gloves are considered in poor taste. Perhaps it's because in movies and novels, the thieves and murderers always wear black gloves.

Lined gloves are most practical, but not so bulky as to make it necessary to remove your glove in order to reach inside your pocket.

Belts

I don't know why women so seldom seem to consider belts when buying a present for a man. I like to choose my own ties, and prefer the ones I select, but a gift belt almost never fails to be appreciated.

Good leather in brown or black with a neat, simple metal buckle is best for wear in the world of business. Belts should be no wider than one and a quarter inches for business suits. Wider ones will not slide through the belt loops of the pants, though they are fine with jeans.

Umbrellas

The kind of umbrella to get depends on how organized you are. If you often leave your umbrella behind in restaurants, taxis, planes, get the cheap standard model, the $4.98 one usually sold by vendors on city streets everywhere you look on rainy days. It doesn't make sense to lose one $25 umbrella after another.

The better-made folding umbrellas are much easier to move around with and less clumsy when not in use, and they can be kept in your briefcase. If classic tradition means a lot to you, get a fine black umbrella with a brown wood handle and hang on to it.

Never let any umbrella be a nuisance. It can be. Some men are always trying out a different umbrella-carrying position every few minutes—in the crook of the arm, over the shoulder like a rifle, grasped by the handle and pointing fore, then aft. They are obviously uncomfortable with the damned things and would be better off getting wet than getting skittish.

In recent years, more colorful umbrellas have been available. Keep their use to nonbusiness occasions.

Protecting Your Investments in the Props of Power

· Suede gloves may be cleaned with stale bread. Put on the glove. Then rub with a slice of stale, dry bread.

· Use diluted hair shampoo for leather gloves that are washable; it won't dry out the leather.

· Before putting gloves away after wearing, blow into them, then pull them out flat. They will look must better for a much longer time.

· To prevent mildew, let your umbrella dry open rather than closed whenever you can.

· Run a damp sponge over the cloth of your umbrella from time to time and it will last longer.

· Use the case that your umbrella comes with for storage. But let the umbrella dry before putting it away.

· It's always better to wind watches forward rather than backward when resetting.

· If you own several watches, but habitually wear only one, wind the others, too, every week or so. This keeps them all in better running order.

· Fabric watchbands are a good idea in summer, as they eliminate the problem of perspiration causing leather to take on an odor. To prevent this with leather watchbands, wax the inside of the band with a neutral shoe polish after cleaning it with a damp, soapy sponge.

8

Putting It All Together for the World of Business

The charts that follow offer some ways of putting clothes together for various situations in the world of business. The occasions are the ones you commonly encounter, from the most formal to the most casual business appointments.

The first set of suggestions is for important, special situations: a late afternoon meeting followed by a business cocktail or dinner appointment; a critical job interview; a top-level, very serious meeting—any time, in short, when you must look your most formal best.

Then come suggestions for the everyday office routine: outside breakfast or lunch meetings; appointments in your office or another man's; the day-to-day business schedule.

The last set of possibilities is for the very casual business situations: a weekend meeting with a client at his home or club; a Friday when you will be leaving the office early for the weekend; a few hours in the office for some catching up on Saturday or Sunday. These are also planned for the man who lives and works in a business or a town where the prevailing atmosphere is fairly casual.

In each case, I have indicated the suit only by a general color from the blue-chip investments best for the world of business. Your navy blue suit might be in hopsacking, flannel, serge, whatever. But the shirt, tie, and so on indicated for a blue suit in the chart will work well for your style category, whatever the fabric of your suit.

Notice that the variations suggested differ very subtly from one style category to the next. But the difference is definite. Playing around with the choices suggested for your category, you can't go wrong. You will express your own view of style in a quiet but unimpeachable way. None of this is meant to lock you into a rigid code. Just to offer a quick and sure reference for looking well dressed without trial and error.

Good Combinations for the Relaxed Classicist of Group A

FOR THE MOST FORMAL BUSINESS SITUATIONS

Suit: Navy blue (probably twill or hopsacking blazer suit)
Shirt: White oxford broadcloth
Tie: Solid maroon silk knit
Belt: Black
Socks: Maroon wool or lisle
Shoes: Black oxfords

FOR EVERYDAY BUSINESS SITUATIONS

Suit: Navy blue
Shirt: Pale blue oxford cloth
Tie: Blue-and-white rep stripe silk
Belt: Black
Socks: Navy blue wool or lisle
Shoes: Black oxfords or slip-ons

Suit: Gray (probably a solid worsted flannel)
Shirt: Blue-and-white pinstripe oxford
Tie: Dark red wool knit
Belt: Black or cordovan
Socks: Maroon wool or lisle
Shoes: Black or cordovan slip-ons or oxfords

The four power styles in the most formal business situations (left to right): Relaxed Classic, Conservative Classic, Elegant Classic, Adventurous Classic.

Suit: Tan (probably a cavalry twill)
Shirt: Gray-and-white striped oxford
Tie: Paisley or geometric in buff, red, and black
Belt: Black or cordovan
Socks: Dark gray
Shoes: Black or cordovan slip-ons or oxfords

FOR THE MOST CASUAL BUSINESS SITUATIONS

Suit: Blue blazer suit (or blazer jacket with gray or tan trousers)
Shirt: Pale yellow oxford or chambray (could also be pale yellow turtleneck)
Tie: Red-and-yellow wool challis paisley
Belt: Cordovan
Socks: Maroon wool or lisle
Shoes: Cordovan slip-ons

Suit: Gray
Shirt: Pale and dark blue box check (maybe with navy or beige V-neck sweater)
Tie: Navy wool knit
Belt: Black
Socks: Navy wool or lisle
Shoes: Black slip-ons

Suit: Tan
Shirt: Blue-and-white or red-and-white gingham check
Tie: Navy or red wool knit
Belt: Cordovan
Socks: Navy or maroon thin wool or lisle
Shoes: Cordovan slip-ons

Good Combinations for the Conservative Classicist of Group B

FOR THE MOST FORMAL BUSINESS SITUATIONS

Suit: Navy blue (probably a solid blue worsted flannel)
Shirt: White plain-collar broadcloth
Tie: Navy-and-white small dots on silk or wool challis

Belt: Black
Socks: Navy lisle
Shoes: Black oxfords

FOR EVERYDAY BUSINESS SITUATIONS

Suit: Navy blue
Shirt: Cream-color oxford
Tie: Club tie with navy blue ground, small bright-colored figures
Belt: Black
Socks: Navy blue lisle
Shoes: Black oxfords or slip-ons

Suit: Gray (probably a solid flannel or solid tropical worsted)
Shirt: Pink oxford
Tie: Red-white-navy striped silk
Belt: Black
Socks: Navy blue
Shoes: Black oxfords or slip-ons

Suit: Tan (probably solid poplin)
Shirt: Blue-and-white spaced fine striped broadcloth
Tie: Slate-blue-and-gray figured silk—paisley or small geometric
Belt: Cordovan or black
Socks: Dark gray fine wool or lisle
Shoes: Cordovan or black oxfords or slip-ons

FOR THE MOST CASUAL BUSINESS SITUATIONS

Suit: Navy blue (or blue blazer with gray or tan trousers)
Shirt: Pink button-down oxford
Tie: Red plaid madras or tartan wool
Belt: Navy webbing belt with brown leather closure; red-and-navy silk ribbon belt
Socks: Maroon or navy blue wool or lisle
Shoes: Black slip-ons

Suit: Gray
Shirt: White, yellow, and black tattersall check (or natural camel turtleneck)

The four power styles in everyday business situations (left to right): *Relaxed Classic, Conservative Classic, Elegant Classic, Adventurous Classic.*

Tie: Dark gray wool or silk knit
Belt: Yellow or red wool webbing belt with brown leather closure
Socks: Dark gray (or bright red or yellow) wool
Shoes: Black or cordovan slip-ons

Suit: Tan
Shirt: Black Watch tartan (of dark green and blue) in miniature scale on cotton
Tie: Navy silk knit (or open collar)
Belt: Cordovan
Socks: Navy thin wool or lisle
Shoes: Cordovan slip-ons

Good Combinations for the Elegant Classicist of Group C

FOR THE MOST FORMAL BUSINESS SITUATIONS

Suit: Navy blue (probably a solid serge) with white pocket square
Shirt: White silky cotton batiste; collar pin
Tie: Slate-and-silver-gray figured woven silk with small pattern
Belt: Black
Socks: Black lisle
Shoes: Black plain or cap-toe oxfords

FOR EVERYDAY BUSINESS SITUATIONS

Suit: Navy blue
Shirt: Pale gray batiste with white collar and cuffs
Tie: Dark-red-and-white small dots printed silk
Belt: Black
Socks: Maroon lisle
Shoes: Black oxfords or slip-ons

Suit: Gray (probably a solid flannel)
Shirt: Pale blue broadcloth
Tie: Black-and-white spaced geometric silk print
Belt: Black
Socks: Black lisle
Shoes: Black oxfords or slip-ons

Suit: Tan (probably solid poplin or a silk-and-wool blend)
Shirt: Pale-pink-and-white pinstripe broadcloth with white collar and cuffs
Tie: Maroon solid silk
Belt: Black
Socks: Maroon lisle
Shoes: Black oxfords or slip-ons

FOR THE MOST CASUAL BUSINESS SITUATIONS

Suit: Navy blue (or blue blazer with gray or light tan trousers)
Shirt: Pale blue cotton (maybe with gray or natural tan cashmere V-neck sweater, or T-neck)
Tie: Tan coarse-weave tweed
Belt: Black
Socks: Brown wool
Shoes: Black slip-ons, brown suede walking shoes, or brown short boots

Suit: Gray
Shirt: White oxford cloth button-down (or natural tan cashmere turtleneck)
Tie: Flag-blue or butter-yellow knit wool tie
Belt: Red felt belt with mahogany-brown leather closure
Socks: Navy blue or maroon thin wool
Shoes: Mahogany brown slip-ons

Suit: Tan
Shirt: Pale pink or blue cotton batiste
Tie: Taupe (gray-brown) dull silk crepe
Belt: Cordovan
Socks: Dark brown
Shoes: Cordovan slip-ons

Good Combinations for the Adventurous Classicist of Group D

FOR THE MOST FORMAL SITUATIONS

Suit: Navy blue (probably a twill blazer suit)
Shirt: White-on-white jacquard broadcloth with geometric figures

The four power styles in the most casual business situations (left to right): Relaxed Classic, Conservative Classic, Elegant Classic, Adventurous Classic.

Tie: Navy silk with narrow woven multicolor stripes
Belt: Black
Socks: Navy
Shoes: Black plain-toe oxfords or slip-ons

FOR EVERYDAY BUSINESS SITUATIONS

Suit: Navy blue (probably twill blazer suit)
Shirt: Pink-and-white minicheck broadcloth
Tie: Dark red silk solid or small self-weave check design
Belt: Black
Socks: Maroon sheer wool or lisle
Shoes: Black slip-ons

Suit: Gray (probably solid tropical worsted)
Shirt: Ivory cotton batiste
Tie: Silk foulard with paisley print in brown, buff, and blue
Belt: Cordovan
Socks: Navy or dark brown sheer wool
Shoes: Cordovan slip-ons

Suit: Tan (probably gabardine)
Shirt: Gray-and-tan hairline stripes on white ground cotton
Tie: Dark gray silk knit
Belt: Black
Socks: Dark gray sheer wool or lisle
Shoes: Black slip-ons

FOR THE MOST CASUAL BUSINESS SITUATIONS

Suit: Navy blue (or jacket from blazer suit, with gray flannels, tan chinos, or faded jeans)
Shirt: Faded blue denim work shirt (or red cashmere turtleneck)
Tie: Red wool knit
Belt: Black or mahogany brown
Socks: Maroon-and-blue argyle pattern wool
Shoes: Black or mahogany-brown slip-ons

Suit: Gray
Shirt: Ivory or ecru broadcloth (maybe with sleeveless V-neck in light ecru)

Tie: Tan silk knit
Belt: Black or mahogany brown
Socks: Brown jacquard tweed pattern sheer wool
Shoes: Black or mahogany-brown slip-ons

Suit: Tan
Shirt: Pale pink voile cotton
Tie: Shantung or linenlike texture with bright multicolor narrow stripes
Belt: Cordovan or mahogany brown
Socks: Maroon or dark blue lisle
Shoes: Cordovan or mahogany-brown slip-ons

Part III

THE WORLD OF LEISURE

9

Investing in Leisure Clothes

Once, a successful man had to work such long hours that he needed little more than pajamas for his off-duty life. Now we enjoy more leisure time and use it in more varied, healthy, and active ways for more pleasure from every moment. We spend more time in active sports, join friends to watch others engaged in active sports. We go dancing all night, and get up early to sail, fish, ski, play tennis or golf. We stay home to work in the garden, paint the bedroom, or cook for friends, or go out to a restaurant, a play, or a movie.

Time spent in the off-hours world may well be the best of your life. Let what you wear express knowledge of that, just as your business clothes express authority, competence, sober skill, and keen precision.

In your off-hours clothing, the principle is pleasure. The clothes to wear are those that make you feel happiest. Dressing for leisure time allows much more freedom than dressing for business; here, personal style can be expressed in much broader ranges of color and pattern, in more varied styling details. Here, too, you can be as creative and up-to-date as you like, as long as it's appropriate for the occasion. That is the general guideline for leisure-time attire. *Dress to fit the occasion.*

Of course, it's frequently difficult to determine exactly what the occasion calls for. How often are you asked to a party and immediately wonder "What will I wear?" Or "What will others be wearing?" Taking your parents-in-law to dinner and the theater, going dancing at an all-night discothèque, having an afternoon barbecue, entertaining at home, accepting the boss's invitation to his country club's black-tie dinner-dance—all these situations call for different clothing choices. To wear clothes that are too informal for a dressy occasion can be acutely embarrassing. I once showed up at a black-tie dinner party in a navy blazer, having mis-read the invitation. The hostess greeted me warmly, but later, I noticed, she switched place cards so that I was seated at the last table instead of next to her at the main table! And showing up overdressed at what turns out to be a casual affair can be equally embarrassing.

Throughout this and the following chapters, I will give some advice about clothing for certain occasions—for black-tie affairs, weddings, funerals, sports, informal or dressy daytime and night-time activities—as well as tips on how to figure out from the in-vitation what to wear. First, though, let's start with the basics.

Blue-Chip Investments for the World of Leisure

To keep your on-hand holdings for the world of leisure as service-able and appropriate as your blue-chip investments for the world of business, begin with the year-in, year-out mainstays: a blazer, a sports jacket, two pairs of slacks. These will take you handsomely through many months of Sundays. Saturdays, too.

FOR THE RELAXED CLASSICIST OF GROUP A

Because his leisure time is apt to be spent in the most out-doorsy way, the Relaxed Classicist should choose rugged fabrics with bold, handsome texture and natural, earthy colorings.

If he already owns a navy blazer (as part of his blue blazer suit) he might not want another. If he buys another blazer it could be in camel's hair or a lightweight rib twist in that color. His sports coat could be Harris tweed, a Scottish District Check tweed, or some other sturdy, decisive plaid. He might also like, especially for warmer weather, a tan bush or safari jacket.

Grayish-tan whipcord or twill slacks would be a good choice for very dressy times, but he will probably get the most use in cool weather from corduroy slacks—oatmeal, British tan, nut brown, or dark gray—or khaki chinos in warm weather. And, of course, blue jeans.

FOR THE CONSERVATIVE CLASSICIST OF GROUP B

Soft, comfortable clothes are important in his off-duty world. He will probably prefer to stay within the framework of classic, muted colors to maintain his look of quiet strength and assurance.

The single-breasted navy blue blazer, in flannel, worsted flannel, or worsted in a year-round weight with gold buttons, is a prized possession for most men of this style group.

For sports coat, clear glen check or overcheck tweeds, brownish tones or grayish ones with dark red or dark blue in the pattern are good choices. The sports coat for warm weather could be a dark plaid or checked cotton (such as a dark madras) or a linen-look jacket in almost any color. Often, though, men in this group wear blue-and-white striped seersucker suit jackets with white or chino trousers rather than investing in a separate summer sports coat, or they wear the navy blazer all year round.

Slacks in cool weather could be gray flannel; in warm weather, tan gabardine or cream flannel. He might also want a pair of mid-wale corduroy trousers in a color that works well with his sports coat.

FOR THE ELEGANT CLASSICIST OF GROUP C

Style and a clean, precise effect are important considerations in his clothes for leisure and business. But greater interest in clothing often leads him to choose (especially for his free time) more adventuresome colors and fabrics. He usually owns more clothes, as well.

His navy blazer is probably almost black, double-breasted, and made of a hard-finish serge or twist. He may also have (or plan to get) a gold-buttoned white blazer for summer, or a cashmere blazer in tan, single-breasted and gold-buttoned.

The silkiest wool or the nappiest is what the Elegant Classicist likes in sports coats. It might also be wide-wale corduroy or smooth cashmere. He may want a very simple windowpane or box plaid in only two colors, or a Harris tweed combining half a dozen colors and tones. It will, of course, be single-breasted if it's tweed, but probably more shaped to the body than men in Group A or Group B would prefer. His "extra" jacket in summer could be white or ecru linen, silk-and-linen (or something that looks like it), or a natural tan safari jacket worn over jeans and a silk shirt.

Preferred slacks are of very fine materials, often cut like jeans. The dressiest of them may (if he has the build for it) have a fairly high waistband with a pleated front, in a very light fawn shade of tan gabardine or a very dark color, even black. Here, as in his business clothes, he looks for luxurious materials and high-key contrasts of color, such as black trousers with an ecru jacket, or vice versa. Perhaps too severe for most men in their off-duty lives, they work well for many men of this group.

FOR THE ADVENTUROUS CLASSICIST OF GROUP D

His world of pleasure is almost invariably full of people actively pursuing a good time. Since his pursuits are seldom solitary ones, he is probably wisest to invest in things that look good in restaurants and nightclubs rather than in more casual, at-home, daytime situations. Often for him, the blazer is a high-priority item.

He probably owns a navy blazer as part of his suit for the world of business. But he will find many occasions to wear a second blazer, since it looks good all day and all night. The best choice might be black, brown, or navy blue velvet. (It should be well made and fit to perfection, though—nothing looks worse than cheap, poorly fitting velvet.) Perhaps the blazer could be in deep bottle green or the darkest maroon. Tan is another thought, but it looks better in the daytime than at night.

His choice for a sports coat would probably have a very definite pattern: herringbone, a windowpane check in brown against a camel ground, or a rich, dark plaid. He might also choose a light, solid-color linen sports coat in white, pale yellow, or blue.

Slacks could be jeans-cut in gabardine, velvet, or pinwale corduroy, or a fine cotton. He might also have a pair of quiet plaid or gun-club check trousers for variety, or maybe a pair of white duck or flannel pants.

Color at Will

Express yourself through your choices. There's nothing hidebound about color for the world of pleasure. Wear any color that gives you a lift. Maybe a scarlet belt or canary-yellow socks, a billiard-green shirt or a turquoise sweater. Whatever you feel happy in. It's probably best, of course, to pack all the brilliant color into one item per outfit unless you really know how to handle color combinations. Yet this is the world in which to indulge a liking for color, any color.

Many men feel happier in less intense, more soothing colors. If you do, fine. You cannot fail to look good if you adapt the quiet, true colors of the world of business to leisure wear. For example: navy polo shirt, tan chino pants, gray wool sport socks, cordovan loafers; white-and-maroon striped shirt, silver-gray cashmere sweater, navy corduroy jeans or white ducks with maroon-and-gray argyle socks and black loafers; or natural tan turtleneck, navy blazer, slate-gray flannel or corduroy slacks, brown wool socks, and cordovan loafers. You can mix any of those elements in any way you like and still come up looking great. Turnouts like these can take you through almost any occasion that comes up in the world of leisure. They have a classic, "landed gentry" appeal, yet they are also money-savers. As in business and travel wear, the so-called neutral colors are always appropriate, and they harmonize well no matter how you combine them. Each item, in a neutral color, can be worn with many more things than the bold color that demands more careful coordinating.

Even if you prefer neutrals, pep them up with some element of strong, happy color. Some men at the most exclusive yacht and country clubs along the East Coast wear, in summer, pants in eye-popping color: canary yellow, cherry red, grass green. But their color formula is to combine these solid, strong-color pants with sober navy blazers, white shirts, striped rep ties, and black polished loafers for parties. It's a particular look for a certain kind of man; not me, but I've seen it often in Southampton and Marblehead.

Also standard for eastern country clubs in summer, Palm Beach or Lyford Cay in winter, is the brilliant, solid-color sports coat (usually linen) of tomato red or banana yellow worn with white trousers, a white or pale-colored shirt, and white buck shoes. This look—bright jacket and pale trousers and shoes—is usually seen on older men.

Your own way with color may have nothing to do with the bright-with-dark or bright-with-light approach. If not, forget it. Use color in the way that feels and looks right to you and those around you.

Here are two fail-safe color tips to keep in mind for the world of leisure. First, any color, any shade—whether pale or intense— gets you farther, looks fresher, and is more becoming when it's a clean, true hue rather than a muddy off-shade. Pale butter yellow and bright canary both have wider appeal and look better on all men than mustard yellow or gold. Not only are such "dirty" colors less apt to complement skin and hair color, but they are also more difficult to coordinate attractively with other colors.

Second, for all casual clothing, from sports coats and ski wear to swimsuits, the classic neutrals (tan, white, gray, wine red, and dark blue) are infallible and versatile choices.

The Power of Pattern

Even when the colors are natural and neutral, pattern can provide the necessary exuberance in clothes for leisure time. Printed or woven, the stripes or plaids can (and should) be bolder and more definite than those for business. Not that a well-dressed man ever wants to look like a bookie or circus barker. You do want your sports coat to look like a *sports* coat, though. It should have a more heavily textured material, or a bolder plaid, than a suit. Something overpowering in a suit might look fine as a sports coat. Sometimes a suit jacket (as a navy blazer, a camel's hair blazer, a tweed suit jacket) can pinch-hit for a sports coat, but generally speaking, suit jackets should be worn only with the trousers that match.

Because the pattern of the sports coat and the trousers worn with it do not match, though, fit is more noticeable than ever. When you wear a matched suit of clothes, people are mainly aware

of overall shape and color; the color is usually fairly quiet and is the same tone from shoulders to shoes. In sports jacket and slacks, there is attention-getting color and pattern contrast. If the jacket's too short or too long, the mistake will show more easily. Bring the same trained eye for good fit to choosing a Saturday jacket that you use to select a suit.

The three best patterns for clothes in the world of leisure are plaids, checks, and stripes. Sometimes, in very well-made casual wear, you may find a good-looking pattern with dots or a repeating, small geometric motif. More often, however, these have a way of looking somewhat cheap. It's hard to make a mistake with plaids, though. From miniature tartans to the most overscaled plaids, they almost invariably have a crisp, masculine style. Checks, too, are usually safe choices. Stripes can be a little trickier. In seersucker and cord stripes, no problem. But awning-stripe blazers recall old productions of *Seventeen* or *The Boy Friend*. Usually the wrong stripe is so obviously wrong that you won't find it except in the lowest-end merchandise anyway. You will find arty and unusual pattterns at every price level, though. Unless you plan to maintain a large collection of casual clothes for very specific occasions, stay away from sports jackets, blazers, and slacks in showy patterns and materials—floral prints, paisleys, abstract and swirling patterns, and anything of damask or embroidered velvet.

Investing in a Blazer or a Sports Coat

Aside from your jeans, the navy blue blazer is the single most adaptable, versatile, and useful piece of clothing you can own for the world of leisure. You can wear it with any nonmatching pants —from jeans to flannels—and look smart and appropriately dressed for anything from a football game to dinner at the most expensive restaurant, from Sunday brunch to a rock concert.

The sports coat (or odd jacket, or extra jacket) is more strictly casual. It can be as quiet (plain natural camel's hair, natural linen, or monochrome tweed) or as loud as you choose in almost any pattern or color that is definitely not one you'd wear for a whole suit (a big plaid tweed in strong colors, a madras plaid, bright solid-color linen). By the way, a blazer can replace this for any occasion, so it isn't necessary to own a sports coat. It's just a nice extra for variety.

Fit. The blazer fits like any suit jacket (details in chapter 3). The sports jacket, especially for cooler weather, should be a little looser so you can wear it over a heavy sweater for knocking around on fall weekends.

Fabric. Blazers are available in everything from heavy wool serge to the lightest-weight tropicals and hopsacking. Pick a weight you can wear pretty much year round—gabardine, light serge, light-weight flannel, for example—since the blazer is right any day of the year. So long as a sports coat doesn't look like the top half of a suit, almost anything goes. Textures—gutsy tweed, crisp heavy linen, homespun, suede, leather—help set it apart from suitings.

A brief word about linen: Once a hot-weather standby, the linen jacket or suit used to be almost synonymous with "wrinkled" and "baggy." Now, though, the rich texture is maintained without as much wrinkling through blending with man-made fibers. Even pure linen now offers longer-lasting shape through manufacturer-applied processes such as ScotchGard. Some linen-look suits and jackets are made entirely of laboratory fibers, though they're probably not as cool to wear as real linen or a blend with a high percentage of natural fiber. Off-white linen (natural ecru, light cream, or ivory) is easier to wear than dead white, which looks somewhat startling and is surprisingly tough to harmonize. White shirts often look dingy next to starch-white linen, and colored ones, unless very pale, look harsh. Nothing looks cleaner, cooler, or more luxurious, though, than an ivory linen jacket or suit with a pale blue or pink shirt and a tie of soft coffee-brown dull-finish silk.

Pale linen suits look impractical (and perhaps ostentatious) for office wear in a big city; however, I know men who work in them on Wall Street. In New Orleans, off-white linen takes the place of a dinner jacket from May through September for some of the city's most prominent men. It depends on where you are, so invest accordingly—and plan on a dry-cleaning after each wearing.

Color and Pattern. Darkest navy blue is the classic, most versatile color for the blazer and is easiest to coordinate. Lighter, brighter blues are trickier to harmonize. Blazers don't have to be navy, though. You may also want a white blazer, a tan blazer—whatever color looks good to you. But first, get navy for maximum use. Gold or silver metal buttons always look good. No law says you have to have them, though; replace metal buttons, if you like, with cobalt-blue enamel ones from a jeweler, tortoiseshell or bone buttons, whatever appeals.

For sports coat coloring, almost anything goes. For a cold-climate jacket, closely study the genius with which the weavers of Scotland use color in tweed. One of the most quietly elegant jackets I have ever seen was of Harris tweed. It was a big plaid with an overcheck. It combined claret red, lavender, and bright red with gray, oatmeal, and dark brown. The effect was subtle, instead of the horse blanket you might imagine.

Style. In any jacket, the more extroverted the color and pattern, the simpler the style should be. Blazers look fine whether they are single- or double-breasted. It's what you feel comfortable with. A tweed jacket is *always* single-breasted; with other sports coats it's a matter of individual choice. If you enjoy tricky style details, the sports coat is the place for them: button-flap pockets, wind-tab buttonholes on the lapel, and so on. Remember, though, you can wear a good tweed for years and perhaps even pass it on to your son. Style tricks have a way of outwearing their appeal long before the tweed wears out. On a recent flight from Los Angeles to New York, I found myself sitting next to John Ryan III, an investment banker. I admired his jacket—a classic tan-and-brown tweed with suede elbow patches and medium-width lapels—and asked him where he'd got it. He pointed out the label and, to my surprise, said he'd had it made in London in 1945.

Investing in Trousers

A good fit is a good fit. But the most flattering fit may be something else again.

Pleated trousers, for instance. These have returned to the style scene in a big way. Many men are reluctant to try them because "they make you look fat." Not necessarily. For a man whose waistline is 30 to 32 inches, pleated trousers can have the visual effect of making his legs look longer and his stomach flatter. For a man whose waistline is larger than 36 inches, pleated trousers can have a functional factor of comfort. It is difficult to say whether pleats will make a man look casually elegant or like a walking pear until he tries them on.

Deciding on details—such as pleated or plain front, pockets, belted or beltless waist—is the major factor in buying pants. There is still fundamental construction to consider, though. It makes a big difference in the way you look in your trousers.

Rise. The rise is the major point to consider in construction. The term refers to the length from crotch to waist. A high rise is usual in dress pants. It is higher on the torso, tighter in the waist and seat. It's more flattering to more men than a low rise, which is usually seen in jeans and sports pants. A low rise looks best on a man with a flat stomach, not too big a behind, and relatively narrow hips. If he is very long-waisted, a low rise can make a man look too long in the torso and too short in the leg.

Waistbands. These come with belt loops or with side tabs. There is no "correct" style. Young Turks who are proud of a 28-inch waistline often like to call attention to it by wearing unbelted trousers. Men with waists above, say, 38 inches have trouble finding belts big enough, so they also like the convenience of beltless trousers. A beautiful belt can also call attention to the waistline, so plenty of physical-fitness freaks insist on belt-loop trousers. Since most belts today fall between one and a quarter and one and three quarter inches in width, the loops should be from two to two and a quarter inches. Very deep belt loops may still be found on some sports pants but look peculiar unless you wear a very wide belt, which isn't in favor right now. Unless a man is very slim-hipped, he should stay away from wide belts when and if they do come back into style.

Pockets. There are a number of ways pockets are treated. Simplest and most common on trousers with suits are the onseam pockets, flush with the outseam of the pants and running vertically. They are fine unless the trousers need a good bit of taking in at the waist or in the seat. Then, onseam pockets tend to stand out like flaps. But if the pants fit as they should to begin with, no problem. Next comes the full-top pocket, two inches below the waistband, and horizontal. It's an informal treatment for sports pants. Hands can be shoved straight down into full-top pockets. The half-top pocket is sometimes called a western pocket. It's on a slant, goes further in toward the thigh, and looks like the pockets on jeans. Finally, the quarter-top pocket, more nearly vertical, but still on a slant, running from under the hipbone down into the outseam. This is one of the most flattering pocket treatments for the male anatomy, whatever condition it is in.

Back pockets may or may not be present on sports pants. In slimline European trousers, the back pockets are often done away with for a cleaner line. In that case, there usually are front pockets, but not always. For a man who wants a close fit but needs someplace for his keys and a little folding money, these pants usually come with a hidden waistband pocket, also called a watch pocket or change pocket. It's a small one just under the waistband.

Trick details—cargo pockets set halfway down the thigh; rings, loops, and other cinches to close the waistband; flaps and buttons on one or all pockets, etc.—are a matter of personal taste and shape. The guy with bowlegs, a bay window, or any other shape problem below the waist should skip such gimmicks on slacks.

Since we discussed trouser length, width, and cuffs in "The World of Business," just a quick recap here.

Cuffs. Trouser cuffs hang straight, parallel to the floor; are about two inches deep; look best on sports trousers with a straight leg;

can make the leg look a fraction shorter than uncuffed trousers would. Trousers without cuffs should fall straight, to cover half the instep in front, and up to three-quarters of an inch longer over the heel. Trousers for suits worn for serious business don't have cuffs; flared trousers, or those with a narrow cut, look better without cuffs.

Width. The width of trouser legs varies. Jeans may be as narrow as 15 inches at knee and cuff; suit trousers today are usually about 19 inches at the knee and 20 inches at the bottom. For a man who wears a higher heel, a 21-inch bottom may provide a better drape over the instep. Very casual trousers may be as narrow in the legs as jeans or wider than trousers for a suit. Don't put a lot of money into trousers with exaggerated shapes, though. I still regret spending a bundle a couple of years ago for custom-made leather jeans with a wide elephant-foot bottom. They were the latest thing then and are still in nearly new condition; but because they were extreme then, they are extremely unwearable now. Don't fight trends; enjoy the ones that go along with what you want your clothes to say about you, but don't make major investments in trendy clothes. You'll be wearing the straight-leg cavalry twills long after the bell bottoms have outworn their amusement value.

Investing in Jeans

A good pair of jeans is an investment in the future because the longer they are worn, the better they look and feel. Three or four years after buying them, jeans will have molded to the body and been washed and worn to a priceless state.

And you can wear them with almost everything you own. Denim jeans with an ivory silk shirt and black velvet jacket make a modern statement that is very elegant, especially with a dark red silk tie and fine boots. Jeans also look super with a fisherman's hand-knit sweater, a plaid flannel shirt, or a button-down shirt and shetland sweater. I can't think of anything I haven't seen worn with blue jeans that didn't look right with them.

Naturally, anything that great is going to be fooled around with by designers. Everybody and his grandmother has attempted to improve on the classic design. Now you can find jeans (or the basic idea) in everything from satin and velvet to hopsacking. No matter how elegant the fabric, a jeans cut still suggests the romance of the frontier, a feel of freedom.

In Europe, jeans have been given a lower rise and a tighter fit. In America, Levi Strauss (having patented the originals in 1873) offers versions now that bear only the vaguest family resemblance to "Levi's."

Great. Jeans are to clothes what potatoes are to dinner. I don't insist on blue denim any more than I would insist on French fries or hash browns every night. Duchess potatoes might be a nice change. Why not velvet jeans?

Check out the variations. See what happens when you put on a French jean with a lower rise and a tighter fit, or a stovepipe jean with a wider leg. You might prefer a zipper fly to the harder-to-find button fly, but you can't know until you try them both.

When you do find a jeans cut that pleases you, buy two pairs at the same time. They will be worn more often than you think, and having two or more pairs of jeans avoids the trauma of breaking in a new pair from scratch and having to get rid of the pair that fits perfectly but is too threadbare to wear.

Authenticity is the name of the game in jeans. The closer a man sticks to classic "blue jeans" styling, whether his jeans are blue or any other color, denim or other material, the better he looks. Braided belt loops, stitched-down pleats over the hips, seams in funny places—there are lots of tricky styling gimmicks used on jeans. For some reason, the more details, the cheaper the look.

Can you wear jeans? Some men don't think so. Usually they are wrong. It depends on the jeans. But stocky men and very thin men must choose carefully. They may have to try on twenty pairs to find one that is flattering, but it's usually possible.

For a very heavy man, jeans should be cut with a full thigh. Narrow straight-leg jeans may make him seem top-heavy. Flares and bell bottoms are not great on him (or anybody else). He should try the stovepipe jeans. And he should avoid fancy pocket stitching and an excess of rivets.

The skinny man should be a natural for jeans—flat stomach, lean legs—but jeans can hang on him and look very baggy in the seat. He owes it to himself to try on imported styles. They are cut on slimmer lines, especially in the seat.

Protecting Your Investment in Trousers

· Hang trousers from wooden bar-clamp trouser hangers whenever possible. Wrinkles and creases will fall out, and there will be no fold line as with regular hangers.

· If you must use a plain wooden bar hanger for trousers, fold one leg over the other so the cuff of one trouser leg falls at the inner crotch of the trousers and the other overlaps it. This will minimize the fold line.

· When forced to use a plain wire coat hanger for trousers, lay a terry towel over the crossbar before putting trousers over it. You risk a sharp hanging crease at the knee otherwise.

· If hangers are in short supply, try hanging trousers over a door frame, then closing the door on them, or draping them (just at ankle level) over the top of a dresser drawer, then closing the drawer. They will hold their shape better than if laid across a chair overnight. Gravity again.

· Before hanging trousers, however you do it, take everything out of the pockets. Take off the belt as well. Extra weight can pull clothes out of alignment.

· When the zipper sticks on trousers, open it and run a pencil up and down the length of the fly. The minute amount of graphite that comes off on the metal will lubricate it. But blow off the excess. If you are heavy-handed, or working with the zipper on light-colored trousers, work on the back side of the zipper. It's just as effective, and there'll be no chance of a pencil smudge on the front of your pants.

Shirts for Leisure Wear

If business shirts should have no more than two colors plus white in a small, fine-lined pattern, leisure shirts can be almost as exuberant as you choose. Multicolor Roman stripes, tartan plaids—almost any color and pattern tastes can be indulged. Still, you don't want to be upstaged by your shirt. Nobody looks his best in a shirt with an eye-popping giant plaid or convict stripes.

Sometimes, there is no difference between shirts for business and shirts for leisure wear. An oxford-cloth shirt with button-down collar is fine in both worlds.

There are times when you may want to wear a tie during off-duty hours. A solid color wool or silk knit usually strikes the right sporty-but-dressed look with a blazer or tweed jacket and the shirt that can be worn with or without a tie.

Best bets for shirts that allow you the choice of wearing a tie or not are these: tattersall checks, tartan plaids, gingham checks, madras plaids, candy stripes, and block stripes. These all have enough character to look good on their own—not as if you had simply kept on the shirt you wore to the office and removed the tie. These patterns are also neat enough to go well with a blazer and with many patterns of sports coat tweeds. Not all tweeds, though. Unless you trust your eye to tell the winning pattern combination, wear a solid shirt with your patterned sports coat. A soft blue, pink, ecru, or yellow should be fine with anything.

There are four basic categories of shirts that make for well-dressed leisure wear.

The tennis shirt or polo shirt. These have been part of the international power look since the 1920s. There are many varieties, but all are of woven cotton and usually in solid colors. Most famous is the one with a small embroidered crocodile appliquéd over the breast. René Lacoste, the great tennis champ of the twenties, was nicknamed "the crocodile" because of his powerful backhand stroke. So the shirt named after him bore his symbol on its front. Descendants of the crocodile can now be found adorned with penguin, lambs, horses, alligators, and so on.

Polo players then and now wore a looser-fitting short-sleeved shirt. For polo, the shirt was usually white, but the polo style is now available in colors and in bold, horizontal woven stripes with a solid collar.

A man can choose these shirts in any color he likes. I have

Four styles of leisure shirt include the tennis shirt (bottom left);
the western shirt (top right); *the lumberjack shirt* (top left);
and the expensive sport shirt (bottom right).

noticed, though, that the most authoritative men everywhere still prefer white, black, navy blue, tan, dark green, maroon, or bright red. But if pink, kelly green, or baby blue is more appealing and looks good on you, that's what you should wear. Steer clear of purple, lilac, brown, gray, mint green, and orange—they are not very becoming colors for shirts, and they alienate many people.

The western shirt. This one may be in blue denim, a strong plaid, or a solid or plaid flannel. The urge to look like a cowboy can be as intense in London or Paris as it is in Arizona. I have seen men buying cowboy shirts in London while dressed in the bowler hats and stiff collars they wear all day as bankers in "The City." My uncle, chairman of the board of Fiat and the best-dressed man I know, relaxes in a denim Levi's shirt.

Basically, the western shirt offers the great appeal of anything designed as a uniform for hard work. It is practical and sturdy, constructed with efficiency rather than show in mind. It is flattering to every man, provided he is in reasonable shape, because it makes the shoulders look broader and the middle narrower.

Getting the most authentic western shirt, whether a plain denim one by Levi Strauss or a fancy "rodeo" style from a western clothing company is usually the best idea. The authentic original is always more forceful-looking than the copy.

The lumberjack shirt. Heavy enough to serve as a jacket, it's a straightforward, button-down-the-front shirt in thick wool. There is usually a big plaid in vivid colors—typically red and black or green and black. A variation of this, in plaid flannel, is lighter in weight and can be worn under a sweater. The flannel versions can be of cotton flannel, or (more luxurious) in Viyella, which is a blend of fine wool and cotton with a very soft hand. The C.P.O. shirt worn in the U.S. Navy and made of dark blue wool with a long tail is much like the lumberjack shirt, but quieter in effect. These shirts are all esteemed for their powerful, "macho" quality.

The expensive sport shirt. This takes many forms; but it is obviously not a shirt to wear with a tie, and it is obviously expensive (it needn't cost a lot, but it must look as if it did). You might also call this the fashion sport shirt because it makes a definite style statement. A shirt of this kind might have very simple lines and be made of a luxurious cloth, such as an intricately printed silk; or it might have unusual styling, such as a pleated and tucked Mexican shirt of a very simple material. It is, however, a distinctive shirt, "dressy" in effect but obviously casual. The fit is easier to describe than the style. If it is meant to be narrow, the shirt fits the body without pinching or flapping. If meant to be loose and full, there's nothing skimpy about it. One test of how expensive the shirt looks is how well details are thought out and applied. Buttons that don't work are tacky details, as are useless, tacked-on epaulets. The decorative details should be working elements. If the shirt is printed in an elaborate pattern of many colors, as is often the case, look for sharp detail and excellent clarity of color.

These shirts are best worn without a jacket and with very simple pants—jeans, duck slacks, velvet, linen, or gabardine trousers—in a related color that won't upstage the shirt. They should be collected slowly. Although they can be fashionable, they don't go out of style. You might find a shirt in Mexico or Hong Kong, wherever your travels take you this year, that will be an enjoyable souvenir of the trip to be worn for years to come. I am still wearing some shirts made of incredible native-printed cottons that I bought more than ten years ago when I was in the Peace Corps in Africa. I don't wear them all the time, but when I do they're pleasant reminders of good times, and because they are so unusual, people still ask where I found them.

You can have more fun with these sport shirts than with many other areas of dress, and almost any color or pattern you like is acceptable. It's one area where a love of purple, or any other color, can have free rein.

Sweaters: Collect Them

I began my clothing business with sweaters, and I have always felt they offered great freedom of expression for both the man who designs them and the man who wears them. The sweater can be

what's called in the trade a "fashion item," bought for novelty's sake and discarded next year. Or it can be a thing you wear and keep for years. Whichever, it should be something you enjoy.

Build a small portfolio of good-looking sweaters. It's the greatest thing to punch up the way you look for the world of leisure. Sweaters cost relatively little but give all the variety and color you could want. Do it your own way. You won't go wrong. You can have sweaters in the subtle shadings of natural fibers—natural cashmere, natural wool and cotton—or the most vibrant dyes—cherry red, violet, chrome yellow. You can buy a heavy sweater to keep you warm, or a sleeveless sweater-vest just to make you look good. You can even wear a sweater in summer and look sane (as long as it's not a turtleneck). Loose-knit sweaters in cotton or cotton-and-linen can look and feel good on a cool June evening at the beach.

To begin a collection of sweaters with the most useful basics, you might have something like this:

1 dark-color turtleneck: maroon, navy, black, brown, or forest green
1 light-color turtleneck: off-white, camel, tan, yellow, or pale blue
1 medium-color crew neck: tan, gray, or other
1 bright-color V-neck, sleeveless: yellow, red or other
1 medium-color V-neck, long sleeves: blue, tan, yellow, gray, or other
1 light-color bulky knit, crew neck or cardigan: off-white or natural

Of course, that's only a basic idea. You might not like (or look good in) turtlenecks. Skip them. You might be able to wear your sweaters into the office. Okay, get more V-necks since they always look good with shirt and tie. This is as individual an area as exists, I think, in a man's choice of clothing.

For the real novelty sweater, synthetics offer a certain price point. They are usually less expensive than wool, and often they look almost identical. But they don't keep you as warm, if that's a consideration, and I find they don't feel quite so good to the touch or last as long. The biggest drawback of synthetics is that they retain odors. Cleaning or washing never gets these out completely. I made sweaters of synthetics when I first went into business, but I was always dissatisfied with them. Now I use only natural fibers or the blends, which are getting better and better. But the choice, again, is up to you.

Protecting Your Investment in Sweaters

· When you take off a sweater, shake it out and spread it flat on the bed for a few minutes. This lets the wool fibers readjust to proper shape.

· Always fold a sweater and store it on a shelf. Never hang it—moisture in the air and wool's natural elasticity will cause the sweater to "grow" and hang out of shape.

· If a sweater develops little pills or balls of wool at points of abrasion, don't pull them off by hand. Try a vigorous downward brushing with a stiff, dry sponge.

· Never pull at a loose thread on a sweater. Both machine-made and hand-made knits can be ruined. But with machine knits, you can sometimes get away with clipping a loose thread at the cuff of the sweater. If in doubt, don't. Take it to a cleaner who advertises reweaving as a specialty of the house.

· For washable sweaters, use your hair shampoo if you have no Woolite or Ivory Flakes available. Shampoo won't strip the natural oils from wool.

· To wash a sweater, always use cool water for both the washing and the rinsing. A change in temperature can cause shrinking.

· A splash of ammonia in the wash water before putting in the sweater can soften water and help remove perspiration from your sweater. A few drops of vinegar in the rinse water can keep the wool soft.

· When you put sweaters away for the summer, wrap them in tissue paper and then in newspaper to discourage moths. Your clothes won't smell of mothballs, and they will be free of holes when you unpack them next fall.

Outerwear

Sure you need a coat to stay warm. But what you need even more is air. Entrapped air does a better job of keeping you warm in cold weather than even the heaviest coat. That's one of the interesting conclusions to be drawn from a U.S. Air Force study. The body is "wrapped" in a very thin layer of still, warm air at all times. Because this air conducts heat poorly, it's a great insulator to keep in your body heat. Several layers of lightweight, loose-fitting clothing provide better insulation than one or two heavy layers. To stay warmest, then, you could start with a layer of thermal underwear, put on a lightweight wool shirt (wool is a great insulator), and add a wool sweater over that. Then your coat can be anything you like, and you'll feel as good as you look. Let the unaware men bundle up like abominable snowmen. You can be warmer than they and look better dressed.

TO LOOK GOOD IN

Coats for the world of leisure provide a lot of leeway for expressing personal style. Wear a reverse-hide shearling coat and feel like a cowboy; a glove-suede fur-lined Eisenhower jacket and feel like a millionaire man-about-town; whatever you like. One of Jacqueline Onassis's friends, Mathias Polakovits, has been seen with her around New York wearing his forty-year-old suede Hungarian shooting coat, an authentic antique lined and trimmed with fur. I can't resist collecting and wearing interesting coats, from good-looking army surplus field jackets to fur. Like belts or sweaters, coats are a free-choice item to have fun with.

Probably the best guideline is not to wear a coat that hits right at the knee, but a little below or above it. A little below makes you look taller. Another flattering coat, provided you are in good shape, is the hip-length jacket, like a denim Levi's jacket. To look taller, a parka or car coat should be on the short side, about the length of a suit jacket.

MATERIAL

Material can be anything from waterproof nylon, cotton, or wool to leather or suede. Nylon is great for wet weather, but I find it uncomfortable to wear because it doesn't "breathe." If you begin sweating in your clothes, wet garments will lose their insulating power to keep you warm. They reverse function, in fact, as the water starts evaporating.

Wool, heavyweight or lightweight, always provides superior insulating properties. Cotton, if you layer clothes under it, can keep you very warm and is always comfortable. Leather is very warm, looks luxurious, and lasts forever. Avoid imitation leather, though—it wears out easily and usually looks cheap. Suede is not as warm as it appears, and it's very delicate, but it looks and feels extremely rich and supple. Both leather and suede require much care and are expensive to clean, but they last a long time if given proper attention.

Shoes

Because we do more things with our time, we need more shoes. We know more about our bodies, so we know that perfect jogging shoes are lightweight and cushion the feet, but tennis demands a different shoe. Either is fine for noodling around in the car, but if you plan to get in a little golf, you need still another kind.

Leisure shoes for sports activities are covered according to specific use in the sports section in the next chapter. Here, let's consider the pure loafing-around shoe.

Espadrilles. The rope-soled canvas slip-ons that are standard on Mediterranean beaches and glossy yachts come in every color. Because of the wide, flat-footed shape of these comfortable shoes, feet look their biggest. You do best to relate the brightness of your espadrilles to the trousers or swimsuit you wear with them. Both vivid, or both light. Grass-green espadrilles and tomato-red linen trousers look great. White linen trousers and sand-color

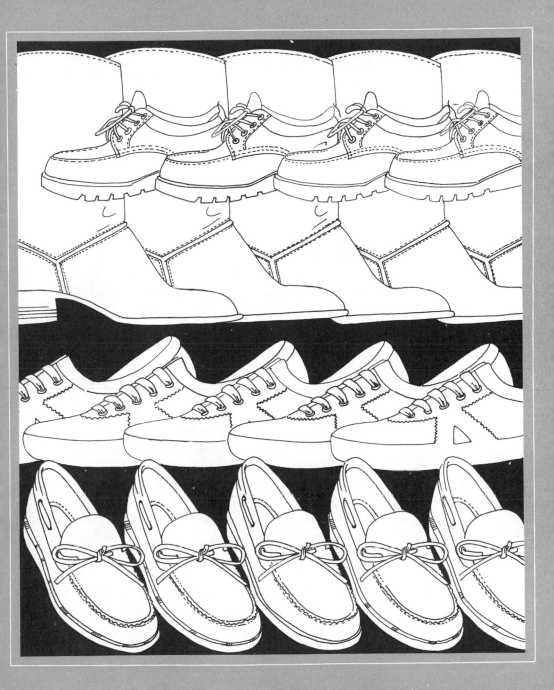

espadrilles look great. But bright green espadrilles and white trousers can make feet look clumsy.

Huaraches. This is the elegant man's sandal. It is woven of thin strips of raw-looking leather in Mexican resorts from Acapulco to Tijuana. Very comfortable to wear, though they tend to creak until broken in. The neutral leather color makes huaraches a good bet with almost any color trousers in summer.

Moccasins. A look at these can show you where the loafer came from. A bead trim on the vamp makes them look closer to the original inspiration—native American footwear. The moccasin has no heel; sole and sides are made of one piece of soft leather, laced around the sides and across the instep with rawhide. A supremely comfortable house shoe, especially when fleece-lined.

Boots

Most boots take their names from the specific sport or occupation for which they were designed. Many are best suited only for that sport. A true knee-high riding boot looks silly worn far from the stable. Though we have all seen men clomping around snowy city pavements wearing ski boots, the men and the boots look ludicrous. For some reason, other boots transcend their original purpose and are very good-looking for "civilian" wear.

Chukka boots. So named for the *chukker,* a period of play lasting seven and a half minutes in a polo match, the chukka boot has lasted in popularity much longer. It is similar to boots worn for the game, and was introduced in 1937 for casual wear by Clarks as the Desert Boot. It's ankle-high, of smooth or suede leather, with a crepe or rubber sole. It looks fine with all sporty clothes.

Construction boots. These are usually yellow ochre or brown leather, ankle-high or mid-calf length, with a cleated rubber sole.

Designed to help workers avoid slipping or twisting their ankles, these boots (usually worn with jeans) have a macho, antiestablishment connotation for many younger men. They are good for country hiking.

Jodhpur boots. These are ideal for wear with wide-hipped jodhpur riding pants. Jodhpur is a former princely state in India. The designs were originally worn only there. When my parents were guests of the Maharajah of Jodhpur in the thirties on their honeymoon in India, photos were taken of the whole boar-hunting party —all in jodhpurs. The style didn't remain in India when the British left, though. It's worldwide today probably because this is the most adaptable boot for everyday wear as well as riding. It reaches just above the ankle, the toe is plain, the heel is relatively flat, and the boot closes with an adjustable strap-and-buckle just over the instep. It is almost always seen in a rich saddle-tan leather that looks good with just about every color found in sports clothes.

Western boots. At its best, the western boot is the greatest manifestation of personal style the American man has devised. The fine examples are truly beautiful, ideally engineered for comfort when riding or walking. It's commonly a mid-calf boot with either scalloped or flat top. The sides, and often the toe, are usually embellished with stitching—subdued or all-out sumptuous. President Johnson always had very plain western boots (when everybody knows you're important you can afford to wear simple styles). Other big Texans go in for technicolor effects in stitching as bright and elaborate as a bullfighter's suit. But all the fireworks go on above the ankle so that they're hidden by the trousers—it's a very discreet way of indulging a taste for the gorgeous. (I've noticed, though, that men who wear these extraordinary boots have a way of putting their legs up, feet on their desks, to offer a glimpse of what's special about their boots.) Toe shapes come in great variety: squared Texas toe, very narrow toe, or wide round western toe, among others. The classic heel shape is the tapered two-inch riding heel. You can also choose the one-inch block heel, or something in between. These boots are usually custom-made, but needn't be. Variations of every sort are available in western and riding shops at all prices. The Frye boot has become very popular in recent years; it's carried in most shoe stores.

Socks

Like sweaters, socks can be an expression of a certain sense of play. I enjoy wearing patterned socks, such as argyles, that have a mixture of colors. You might also like solid-color sports socks in bright red or green. Yellow ones can look terrific as a bright touch of color with brown loafers, gray flannels, and a sweater and tweed jacket in brownish tones; then the socks give a little fun to the quiet get-up. Heavy white cotton athletic socks are a classic American choice with sneakers. Unless recommended by your doctor for a foot ailment, don't wear white socks with any other shoes.

Scarves

There is a character that is almost national about scarves. The French wear them often, and they like all kinds, from great long ones to wrap around the neck to short ones that they hang across the back of the neck and down into the front of a jacket or blazer. The Italians and Germans seldom wear a scarf unless they are bundled against the cold, and then it's a pretty conservative short woolen muffler. The English use mufflers, if they wear scarves at all. Americans, I find, appreciate the practicality of their warmth as well as the style potential of scarves. In New York, especially, well-dressed men will often pull a wool knit or tweedy scarf across the back of the collar of a tweed jacket and tuck it in between jacket lapels and the sweater, just for the additional interest this kind of layering gives. Sure, it can also keep them warmer, but that isn't the real point. Having a little fun with clothes is.

Sunglasses

Dark glasses *are* for practicality. That the right sunglasses can also be a great asset to your looks is a nice bonus. But select any glasses for eye comfort first.

Whether you wear prescription sunglasses or not, you should wear them whenever you're out in the open. They are an effective shield against polluted air, against wind-borne particles that can injure the eye. After a sunny day without sunglasses, your night vision is cut by 50 percent, and your chances of eventually developing cataracts are far greater if you habitually go out in the sun without dark glasses. For a really sunny day on the beach, use *dark* glasses: those that filter out 75 to 85 percent of the light. Under normal conditions, such as driving, playing golf, being out-of-doors around town, there isn't as much reflected glare as at the beach. Then sunglasses should block only 70 percent of the light, but they should still be dark. Don't, however, wear dark glasses indoors or to cut the glare while driving at night. They don't really harm your eyes, but they do tire them more. Tinted glasses are the best idea for softening glare. These absorb from 10 to 20 percent of the light. If you don't want to bother changing your glasses every time you go into different light, investigate the lenses that darken automatically as the light brightens. They are almost clear indoors, dark in ultraviolet light outdoors. Then you need only one pair of sunglasses to protect your eyes adequately.

You can find lenses in almost any color. Gray and green are least distorting when you look through them at other colors, so they're easiest on the eyes. Yellow lenses look very racy, but have specialized use. Driving in the fog, or playing tennis on cloudy days or in night lighting, they increase contrasts and sharpen details. They're great then, but not for cutting glare from the sun. It is said, too, that they are fatiguing if worn for a long time. For some reason, brown lenses make the eyes behind them look very tired. You'll see what I mean if you look through a sample lens at the optometrist's or dispensing optician's. First try brown, then switch to gray and see how much more alert the eye appears.

Speaking of the optometrist and optician, that's who you

should see for sunglasses. You will be sure of getting the proper lens for the proper purpose, and you can have the frames correctly fitted. Of course, if you wear prescription glasses, there is no other choice than to get your glasses from an optometrist. But even if you don't wear prescription sunglasses, I think you still should get first-rate glasses, which you will usually find at a specialist's store.

If you want to save money by picking up sunglasses off the rack in a drugstore or supermarket, check them carefully before you buy. Here's the way: Hold glasses by their temple, and turn them so the lenses are facing up toward the ceiling. Locate a reflection in the lenses; an overhead light fixture is good. Now slowly move the glasses from left to right, tracking the reflection in the lens. If you see any distortion as the reflection goes from one edge of the lens to the other, don't buy them. You won't save money with those glasses, you'll just be throwing them—and good vision —away. Try to find good, ground-glass lenses, or good plastic ones with no distortion.

The frame and side pieces should be joined with a screw, not a pin. If the frame is plastic, side pieces should be reinforced with metal so they will be strong and adjustable for the best fit. Side pieces should be relatively narrow, too. Those more than half an inch wide are dangerous. They block side vision, which could be fatal for a driver, or a pedestrian for that matter.

Shape of the frame should be whatever looks good on you. The classic "aviator" frames seem to look good on just about everybody. But don't restrict your thinking to them. Having recently designed a line of frames myself, I know there is plenty to choose from that is good-looking and new. Whatever sunglasses you choose, be sure to wear them outdoors. You'll look and see better.

Belts

The belt you wear with leisure clothes can be as beautiful and elaborate as an American Indian concho belt of incised silver and turquoise, or as simple as a brass-buckled webbing belt from the army surplus store. It's a great area for a man to indulge himself by wearing his own brand of fun. Leisure-world belts are taste around the waist, and fantasy in a restrained way. You can have a Hussar's belt or a cowboy's, a classic Ivy League striped elastic belt with leather closings. You can even make your own belt as Fred Astaire used to do, by tying a silk scarf around your waist. Unless you have Mr. Astaire's super brand of elegance, you might look a little strange in that. But if you're game, why not?

The only guideline I might suggest here is that the larger your waist, the narrower the belt should be and the less riveting to the eye. But for a man who keeps his midsection under 36 inches, just about anything goes in belts.

10

What to Wear to What

How to Interpret an Invitation

Remember President Carter's inaugural parties? Word got around that this was to be a "blue jeans inaugural." There was a minor panic in Washington; men accustomed to deciding national policy became indecisive about their own clothes. What to wear became An Issue. The protocol of black or white tie had always made dressing for the diplomatic life a snap. Now dressing for a dinner or party at the White House was suddenly as much an open question as it can be everywhere else in the country.

How can you tell how literally an invitation to "come as you are" is meant? What does "casual" mean when you're invited to the boss's home for dinner? What's right for an "informal" dance at the country club? Is "no tie" just that? We all miscalculate at least once. I and everybody else I know has had the embarrassment of showing up in jeans to find all the other men in dark suits, or vice versa. How to handle it when that happens?

Easy. If you dress inappropriately, just relax and enjoy yourself. Try to be the kind of guest a hostess would want to have at her party whether he was in white tie or overalls. Especially if you don't know the other guests, you should make a slightly greater than usual attempt at being friendly and outgoing.

You wore jeans and they didn't? So you look more casual, relaxed, and open—act accordingly. You dressed in black tie and they didn't? That suggests you consider this a special, rather gala occasion, so behave in your most ingratiating "party" manner.

In no event should you begin to change clothes on the spot—asking to borrow a tie from the host, or stripping down to open-neck formal shirt and tux trousers. You then look half-dressed or badly put-together and call attention to a miscalculation that would otherwise be ignored. No elaborate apologies or explanations, either. Nobody wants to hear about your imaginary suitcase lost through airline negligence.

There is a certain pattern to what goes that you can gather from invitation phrasing. In my experience:

"Come as you are" means the hostess is hoping her party will be very relaxed and give her guests a chance to be their most unpretentious. It's a free-for-all, and the one time to leave the blazer in the closet. Go in jeans and a sweater or polo shirt, or wear the wild shirt you bought in Mexico, or almost anything that suggests getting into the spirit of a nondressy party.

"It's informal" is much trickier. In a big city, or with the hostess who usually has the kind of supper-dance thing where men come in black tie, this probably means wear a business suit or navy blazer and gray flannels. You can't go wrong with those. In the evening, though, it's probably a good idea to switch to a white shirt and a tie with a somewhat sprightlier pattern than you might have worn to the office—a small paisley in bright colors, navy-on-yellow polka dots, or red-on-white dots—if you wear the dark or chalkstripe suit. In some other situations, "informal" means "relaxed," and you can't go wrong with a good-looking sport shirt open at the neck, blazer, and slacks.

"Very casual" is another party time when the blazer is handy. Instead of flannels, though, blue jeans with it, or any other definitely leisure-time, well-cut pants. If the weather is warm, wear a rich-looking shirt that is definitely not one you'd wear with a tie, and a belt with a handsome buckle.

"No tie" depends, as always, on the hostess and how she usually gives a party. According to the season, though, I would wear: navy blazer, open silk shirt, white ducks or gray flannels or jeans. Or tweed sports coat, corduroy slacks or cord jeans, and either turtleneck or open tattersall check shirt under V-neck sleeveless sweater or crew-neck sweater. Or tan safari jacket with sleeves rolled up to the elbow, over an open shirt or turtleneck sweater, and jeans. It sounds repetitious, maybe, but if you don't know the territory, go for the blazer.

Black Tie Nights

Once I went to the movies in Palm Beach. The film was all about "high society" in New York. Most of the audience was made up of exactly the sort of people being portrayed. When the leading man wore a white dinner jacket in one scene, there were reactions from chortles and chuckles to guffaws from the audience. I think white jackets look cool and fine in hot weather, but not everyone does. Unless you know your audience in advance, and are sure it will always be the same, buy black.

The one suit that is always correct for black-tie occasions is a good-fitting black tuxedo. The classic tux outfit goes: black tuxedo of flat, year-around but not shiny material, with satin lapels; black "butterfly" bow tie of dull-finish silk crepe, faille, or satin (the ready-tied bow on a neck band is indistinguishable from the tie-it-yourself ones, while clip-ons are less successful); white evening shirt with knife-pleat bosom, closed with shirt studs and matching cuff links of white or yellow gold, platinum, onyx, or mother-of-pearl; white or black suspenders; black satin cummerbund to match lapels; black silk socks, thin and unribbed; and black patent-leather dancing pumps with grosgrain bow.

That outfit is partially flexible. The lapels and cummerbund might be flat rather than shiny satin. Wing collars might appeal to men in Groups B and C. And you might prefer plain-toe oxford shoes in black calf or black patent leather. In fact, many men find classic dancing pumps rather foppish. I once overheard two aides of then-governor Reagan discussing their boss at a Los Angeles party: "The governor looks great in a tuxedo, doesn't he?" "Yeah, but did you catch those Dolly Shoes?" If he's less secure in his masculinity than Ronald Reagan is, a man might be less comfortable in "Dolly Shoes."

The one invariable rule, though: Always wear white shirt with black tux. You might find other men in light blue, but don't let that throw you; if you're the only one in white shirt at a black-tie affair, then you're the only one correctly dressed.

The next step down in formality from the black tux is the black dinner suit. In fact, if you don't own a tux and aren't prepared to buy one, you'll usually do as well with a plain black suit as with a rented tux. Rented tuxedos rarely fit well and often look pretty tacky. If you can't find one that makes you look your best—which, after all, is the point of getting so dressed up—then I'd suggest wearing a plain black suit instead. Gabardine is a good material, or perhaps a perfectly fitting black velvet. With the suit, wear a plain white cotton broadcloth or silk shirt and a black butterfly bow tie, a black leather belt (no cummerbund or suspenders), black socks, and black plain-toe leather oxfords.

White Tie

White tie means a full-dress evening suit. It is rarely worn today except at debutante cotillions and some very grand, very traditional balls. The private Mardi Gras balls in New Orleans are white-tie affairs.

If you are going to a white-tie occasion, I suggest renting the outfit well in advance to allow time for any necessary alterations to be made. The whole rig is for hire at larger formal-wear specialists. It consists of a black cutaway tail coat, black trousers, white piqué waistcoat, white wing-collar shirt, and white piqué butterfly bow tie. Shoes and socks are the same as for black tie.

Weddings

The groom is, of course, indispensable, but what he wears is generally up to the bride. This is her big day. She is the star, and what she says usually goes. Your fiancée might have looked at magazines like *Bride's* and *Modern Bride* for ideas. Men in their editorial photos and ads are often wearing the most eccentric versions of "formal" clothes: Riverboat Gambler, Edwardian Fop models in white, candied-almond pastels, and more. Most men look festive, striking, but somewhat uncomfortable in fancy dress of this kind. If it just doesn't suit them, they know it and show it. So although the bride calls the shots, discuss it. She loves you. You can probably work out something that suits you both.

The barefoot wedding of a few years ago seems to have faded out along with the flower children. Now, ceremonies tend to be traditional again. The traditional way to dress for it is worth running over here.

Elaborate daytime wedding. The groom, the best man, and the ushers dress identically (except that the groom wears a more elaborate white boutonniere in his lapel). They all wear morning coat in black or gray; dark gray striped trousers; white shirt; black-and-white dot or stripe silk tie; black, white, or gray vest; black silk socks; black shoes; and white boutonniere. Of course, nobody owns a morning coat and striped trousers anymore, so these would all be rented. The cutaway morning coat with tails is pretty tricky to wear and makes most men even more uncomfortable than those fancy mint-green damask numbers. The so-called club coat (same as a cutaway tailed jacket but without the tails) is better for most fellows.

Simpler daytime wedding. All the men of the wedding party wear dark blue suit, white shirt, gray-and-white or blue-and-white tie, white boutonniere. For a summer wedding, especially in the country, navy blazer, white flannel slacks, white boutonniere, and blue-and-white tie is traditionally correct.

Evening wedding. Groom, best man, and ushers should wear the same clothes as to a formal evening dance: either black tie and dinner suit or, if the wedding is very elaborate, white tie and tails.

But neither tuxedos nor tailcoat and white tie are appropriate traditional choices unless the wedding is held after six o'clock.

Guests. No matter how simple or elaborate the wedding, whatever time of day or year, guests cannot go wrong with the blue-chip navy suit. That's also the groom's best choice for a second or third marriage.

Funerals

A plain dark suit, white shirt, and invariably a black four-in-hand tie should be worn to a funeral (and the tie reserved for funerals only).

Power Plays: What to Wear for Active Sports

Active sportswear has become, over the past decades, more and more diverse and flexible, and in turn has greatly influenced non-sportswear styles, so that the line between the two has blurred. And because so many people have taken up active sports in the past few years, clothes once confined to the tennis court or the jogging track are now seen on the street, in stores, all over the place.

Still, there are traditional guidelines, some of which must be adhered to in certain clubs and some of which should be followed if only to look right with the people who care about the differences.

The most efficient gear always looks the best. If you are a serious sportsman, you already know what works best for you. That's what you should wear. But with leisure time growing, there are increasing numbers of men who consider taking up yet another sport. The following is a quick rundown to alert you to some of the checkpoints for authentic equipment for some of the more popular games and pursuits.

Boating. The real sailor is really casual. He'd rather scrape barnacles than wear anything with a "nautical" motif—shirts with little anchors or pennants. Preferred clothes for a boat—12-meter

sloop, sunfish, or stinkpot—are: rubber-soled Sperry Topsider moccasins, cotton sports pants (chinos, white ducks, jeans, or cords), cotton polo shirt. If it's cool, a crew-neck shetland or fisherman's sweater. Foul-weather gear, waterproof slickers, and windbreakers are a good idea. Best color range anywhere around the water is navy blue and white or khaki. Signal yellow or orange for slickers always looks good, too. Once the sun is over the yardarm, many sailors change for parties on deck or at the yacht club. It's usual to wear a white polo shirt, topsiders just as in the daytime, a navy blazer, and white, tan, or bright solid-color linen trousers.

Golf. Go easy on the golfing emblems and insignia. Many men, when duffers, buy all kinds of gadgety things to wear for the game, everything emblazoned with a top pro's signature or coy prints with golf tees and such. A little of this is okay, but keep it to a minimum. Men with the lowest par at the most prestigious golf clubs generally wear clothes that would look fine and be comfortable off the course or on: chinos or corduroys or other sport slacks, good sweater and open shirt or a polo shirt, and brown golf shoes. At the jazzier clubs, you see more color and sharper coordination. If that's the style of your club, or if it gives you a psychological edge to play in green-and-white shoes and chartreuse golf slacks, go ahead. You're out there to enjoy yourself.

Racquet Games: Platform Tennis, Racquetball, Squash, Tennis. Alphabetically the last, tennis is certainly the first in popularity, and the fastest growing sport in the country. More than twelve million players at this writing, and even more people signing up for lessons daily. Every one of them can look like a champ in tennis whites—white shorts and white cotton pullover short-sleeved tennis shirt. Pastel shorts and shirts are acceptable at some clubs, but not allowed at many—and not worn by most longtime players. You can't go wrong, though, whether you play with a $150 graphite racquet or a $5 wooden one, when you wear white.

Tennis whites are the standard for squash, as well. Have a sweater handy to prevent muscle chill after play. The classic is a white cablestitch V-neck or cardigan trimmed with a band of maroon and a band of navy blue.

Racquetball is played in just about anything that comes to hand, but tennis whites have a championship-class look for this game, too.

Platform tennis was originally developed as a cold-weather stand-in for tennis, so the players' clothes are usually warm: corduroys or jeans and a sweater with tennis shoes. When the weather is really cold, some players add a sleeveless vest of down-filled nylon or a ski parka.

One vital thing to wear, whatever the racquet game, is some eye protector. Writing in the *Journal of the American Medical Association*, opthalmologists Dennis B. Freilich and Morton H. Seelenfreund detailed a series of cases of severe retinal damage to players who did not wear protective devices. They suggest a handball eye protector or sports sunglasses made with impact-resistant lenses and metal or plastic side pieces that curl around the ears. Yellow lenses can even help your game if you play under night lights or on cloudy days. They sharpen contrast, so you see the ball better. If you see it headed your way, it's traveling at an average speed of 60 miles per hour. If it's aimed at your eye, duck.

Water Sports. It is a point in his favor that the American man never adopted the bikini. But the bathing suit doesn't have to be as baggy as it often is. If you are in swimming trim, a nylon racing suit in black or navy looks great. If you are somewhat out of shape at the start of the summer, wear a boxer or gym-shorts model (and consider going to the gym, too). Whichever style, try to get it in nylon. Aside from skiwear, swimwear is the only kind of clothing for which I think synthetic fibers are ideal. Who wants to pack a wet cotton swimsuit, or sit around in one while it dries? If you are dark, any color swimsuit looks good. If you're pale, you are better off with soft shades of medium tone. Faded denim blue is just about ideal. If you're trying to minimize extra poundage, don't wear a very dark color, such as black, or a very light one, such as white. Either makes for a severe silhouette, very noticeable against sea and sky. Soft gray-blue or khaki blends more easily into the surroundings. If you are really out of shape, get a long white terrycloth robe and wrap up in it when you come out of the water. That's the way it's done in the very chic European resorts. It also protects you from the pain and aging effects of sunburn. If a long robe has too much the look of Deauville decadence to suit you, use a short terry kimono, a Cuban wedding shirt, or a safari jacket. Anything but a cabana jacket that matches your swimsuit.

Skiing. You may have just decided to join the skiers. It's my favorite sport, and I have been at it since I was three. We lived for part of each year at Cortina d'Ampezzo, so I had lots of opportunity to become a very good skier. If you are just beginning, though, you are probably tempted to first equip yourself with the best skis and ski clothes to give yourself a head start. Don't. Two reasons. First, you will probably learn by the GLM (graduated length method) at most resorts. That means you start out on very short skis, and it takes a while to graduate to the standard size. Second, nothing is so laughable to the expert skier as the kind of "snow bunny" who shows up dressed like Jean-Claude Killy, with eye-catching clothes and equipment, but heads for the beginner's slope, or worse, can't figure out the rope tow. First few times out, rent. When you're ready to buy, plan on spending about $200 or $250 for skis, bindings, boots, and poles.

Ski fashions change from year to year and from place to place. In Europe, the style has always been to wear black or another dark color, usually with a fur parka and mittens. In the United States, skiers have traditionally been more colorful, with electric-blue, orange, or another bright color for pants and parka. Now, as in every other area of life, ski style is becoming international. It's becoming more democratic, too; you fit in and look good anywhere in the world when you ski in jeans, so you needn't blow a lot of cash on the most expensive, latest ski clothes.

You never look good if you are shivering, though. Again, layering is your best bet. In the coldest weather, start with Roylon longjohns if you can find them. If not, you might try dancer's leotards, with feet. Over them, wear thermal underwear and wool knee-high socks, topped with straight-leg jeans. To stay warm above the waist, wear thermal underwear tops, then a cotton turtleneck, flannel shirt, and wool sweater. Top it with a good-looking parka. In warmer weather, omit layers as you like.

You do need gloves, and two pairs are better than one. At some shops (not all) you may be able to find silk liners. These superthin silk gloves, worn under ski mittens or gloves, are very good for keeping hands warm. If you don't come across silk liners, buy knitted wool gloves to wear under the top pair.

Riding. To wear the right thing, you have to know the territory. I, and most people I know, wear jeans nowadays for riding wherever we are. But in Europe, in some parts of the East Coast, and especially in South America, there are a number of riders who still prefer jodhpurs. Many of us wear western boots for riding, because it's easy to hook the big heel into the stirrup. It's really up to personal taste, and beautiful English riding boots are wonderful. Jodhpur boots are, like western ones, useful and attractive for wear even when there isn't a horse for miles around. For further information, send for a catalog from Millers (see the appendix).

Running. Everybody seems to be running and jogging now, and the only equipment that's crucial is the shoe. You can wear ordinary loose clothes, a sweat suit, a spiffy warm-up suit to match your shoes, or gym shorts and a T-shirt. The shoe's the thing. You'll have to spend at least $20 to $25 for a good shoe. John Weiss, owner of Runner's World, a Manhattan sporting goods store that specializes in running shoes, advises that beginners, especially, need the best running shoe. Here's what to look for: raised heels (more air in the rubber, hence softer on the foot); hollowed heels that cup the foot; the proper tread on the sole. Proper tread means the ridges of the rear sole should angle toward the front to grip the ground on downhill runs, front ridges should angle toward the back to aid you in going uphill; solid ridges on the sole can help prevent slipping if you run in mud or wet grass. Except for competition, wear training shoes that weigh 12 or 13 ounces. These are sturdier and more comfortable. Racing shoes, right for a marathon run, weigh about half that. In case you've ever wondered about the difference—jogging is generally defined as doing a mile in eight minutes or more, running as doing the mile in less. With the right shoes, you'll feel like a runner, no matter what the stopwatch says.

11

Putting It All Together for the World of Leisure

You call your own shots in dress as in every other facet of your world of leisure. Occasionally, though, we all face a problem of what to wear. Following are some tips for men of each style grouping as to appropriate clothing possibilities for some of the fairly standard leisure situations. (I have not included more formal situations since they are covered in chapters 8 and 10.) Though the activity of the day or evening might be typical, there can be a question of what to wear—especially off your own turf, when you're traveling for business or pleasure. What I've suggested are the kinds of things I see on men of power all over the States and in Europe. You shouldn't go wrong with any of these anywhere. You may use them as quick reference when in doubt, or adapt them and substitute freely to suit your mood, taste, or particular situation. The general idea of these clothes plans is to help clarify your thinking as to your own ways of putting it all together for the world of leisure.

The four power styles at an outdoor party (left to right): *Relaxed Classic;*
Conservative Classic; Elegant Classic; Adventurous Classic.

Good Combinations for the Relaxed Classicist
of Group A

FOR A BRUNCH, PICNIC, OR AFTERNOON OUTDOOR PARTY

Jacket (if worn): Brownish tweed sports coat
Pants: Tan corduroy, or blue jeans
Shirt: Blue denim western shirt, or beige turtleneck
Belt: Brown leather
Socks: Gray wool
Shoes: Brown moccasins or loafers

FOR CASUAL DRINKS-AND-DINNER AT THE HOME OF FRIENDS

Jacket (if worn): Plaid sports coat in brownish tones
Pants: Tan cavalry twill or gray worsted flannel
Shirt: Yellow flannel or dark red turtleneck
Belt: Brown leather
Socks: Brown or dark red wool
Shoes: Brown short boots

Jacket: Tan corduroy sports jacket
Pants: Gray worsted flannel or tan cavalry twill
Shirt: Red-and-white candy-stripe oxford cloth or red turtleneck
Tie (if worn): Red wool knit
Belt: Brown leather
Socks: Maroon wool
Shoes: Brown short boots

FOR AN INFORMAL DANCE AT A CLUB, OR A
DINNER-AND-THEATER DATE

Jacket: Navy blazer suit
Pants: Matching suit pants, or gray worsted flannel
Shirt: White oxford cloth
Tie: Multicolor striped silk
Belt: Black leather
Socks: Navy blue thin wool
Shoes: Black slip-ons

FOR LATE-NIGHT DISCO DANCING

Jacket (if worn): Dark brown suede western jacket
Pants: Black corduroy or blue denim jeans
Shirt: Chocolate-brown or black cotton turtleneck
Belt: Black leather with handsome buckle
Socks: Black thin wool
Shoes: Black slip-ons

Good Combinations for the Conservative Classicist of Group B

FOR A BRUNCH, PICNIC, OR AFTERNOON OUTDOOR PARTY

Jacket (if worn): Navy blazer or brown tweed jacket
Pants: Tan chinos, or light tan corduroy
Shirt: Pink polo shirt
Belt: Brown-and-red striped webbing
Socks: Gray wool or cotton sport socks
Shoes: Brown loafers or topsiders

FOR CASUAL DRINKS-AND-DINNER AT THE HOME OF FRIENDS

Jacket (if worn): Navy blazer
Pants: Gray flannels or tan chinos
Shirt: White oxford button-down, V-neck yellow sweater, or camel turtleneck
Belt: Black leather
Socks: Navy thin wool
Shoes: Black slip-ons

Jacket: Navy blazer
Pants: Gray flannel or tan poplin
Shirt: Blue-black-white tattersall
Tie (if worn): Solid navy silk knit, or club tie
Belt: Black leather
Socks: Navy wool
Shoes: Black slip-ons

The four power styles at a casual evening with friends (left
to right): *Relaxed Classic, Conservative Classic, Elegant Classic,
Adventurous Classic.*

**FOR AN INFORMAL DANCE AT A CLUB, OR A
DINNER-AND-THEATER DATE**

Jacket: Navy blue blazer
Pants: Dark gray flannel
Shirt: White oxford button-down
Tie: Navy-red-white rep stripe silk, or solid navy silk knit
Belt: Black leather
Socks: Maroon or navy blue thin wool
Shoes: Black slip-ons

FOR LATE-NIGHT DISCO DANCING

Jacket (if worn): Navy blazer
Pants: Wine-red corduroy
Shirt: Open-collar white or pink silk
Belt: Black leather
Socks: Maroon or navy
Shoes: Black slip-ons

Good Combinations for the Elegant Classicist of Group C

FOR A BRUNCH, PICNIC, OR AFTERNOON OUTDOOR PARTY

Jacket (if worn): Navy blazer
Pants: Tan cavalry twill, white flannel, or white duck
Shirt: Blue-and-white striped polo shirt
Belt: Navy braided cord
Socks: Navy thin wool or lisle
Shoes: Brown slip-ons, or (without socks) white espadrilles

FOR CASUAL DRINKS-AND-DINNER AT THE HOME OF FRIENDS

Jacket (if worn): Maroon velvet blazer
Pants: Gray flannel or black gabardine
Shirt: Pink cotton voile, perhaps with printed red silk ascot in open collar
Belt: Black leather
Socks: Maroon thin wool or lisle
Shoes: Black slip-ons

The four power styles at a club dance or theater date (left to right): *Relaxed Classic, Conservative Classic, Elegant Classic, Adventurous Classic.*

Jacket: Gray-black-and-white Prince of Wales plaid sports coat
Pants: Gray flannel
Shirt: White broadcloth or gray turtleneck
Tie (if worn): Solid maroon wool knit
Belt: Black leather
Socks: Maroon or dark gray thin wool
Shoes: Black slip-ons

FOR AN INFORMAL DANCE AT A CLUB, OR A DINNER-AND-THEATER DATE

Jacket: Navy blue blazer
Pants: Gray or white flannel
Shirt: White batiste
Tie: Navy-and-white small dots on silk
Belt: Black leather
Socks: Navy thin wool
Shoes: Black slip-ons

FOR LATE-NIGHT DISCO DANCING

Jacket: Black velvet
Pants: Black jeans-cut gabardine
Shirt: Black silk open-neck crepe-de-chine or black silk knit turtleneck
Belt: Black leather
Socks: Black cotton lisle
Shoes: Black slip-ons

Good Combinations for the Adventurous Classicist of Group D

FOR A BRUNCH, PICNIC, OR AFTERNOON OUTDOOR PARTY

Jacket (if worn): Navy cardigan sweater, or natural suede windbreaker
Pants: Blue denim or white sailcloth jeans
Shirt: Blue-white-yellow plaid or checked shirt, or turtleneck in camel or navy
Belt: Yellow webbing
Socks: Navy wool
Shoes: Brown moccasins

The four power styles at a late-night disco scene (left to right): *Relaxed Classic, Conservative Classic, Elegant Classic, Adventurous Classic.*

FOR CASUAL DRINKS-AND-DINNER AT THE HOME OF FRIENDS

Jacket (if worn): Tan poplin safari jacket, sleeves rolled
Pants: Black velvet jeans
Shirt: White silk, open and perhaps worn over black cotton lisle turtleneck
Belt: Mahogany brown leather
Socks: Maroon sheer wool or lisle
Shoes: Mahogany-brown or black slip-ons

Jacket: Camel-color blazer
Pants: Navy blue gabardine
Shirt: Ivory silk, or off-white turtleneck
Tie (if worn): Medium brown silk knit
Belt: Mahogany brown leather
Socks: Dark brown thin wool
Shoes: Mahogany brown slip-ons

FOR AN INFORMAL DANCE AT A CLUB, OR A DINNER-AND-THEATER DATE

Jacket: Navy blue velvet blazer
Pants: Navy blue gabardine
Shirt: Ivory silk
Tie: Steel-gray or soft solid red-pink silk crepe
Belt: Black leather
Socks: Dark gray or maroon lisle
Shoes: Black slip-ons

FOR LATE-NIGHT DISCO DANCING

Jacket: Pale natural suede Eisenhower or blouson jacket
Pants: Close-fitting fawn-colored gabardine or white pinwale corduroy
Shirt: White cashmere V-neck sweater with sleeves pushed up, or white silk shirt, sleeves rolled up
Belt: Light tan leather
Socks: Tan cotton lisle
Shoes: Light tan slip-ons or boots

Part IV

THE WORLD OF TRAVEL

12

Travel Clothing and Luggage

Can you really distinguish between a "business trip" and a "pleasure trip"? I can't. To me, any chance to travel is a pleasure, whether or not business is the reason for the journey. There is the pleasure of meeting new people, of seeing different places and different ways of doing things, of eating different foods. And travel helps you to see things with a valuable new perspective on returning home.

To get the most out of the world of travel takes organization. It also helps to plan carefully and to allow for changes in plan. Expect them, go with the flow, and you will seem like a seasoned traveler everywhere you go.

The most important question about any trip is what to take and how to carry it. Of course you don't want to take a lot with you. You don't have to, no matter what your travel plan is.

What to Take

Two years ago I went around the world for a month on a combination business and pleasure trip. I left from Paris in November. Before winding up the trip in New York in December, I went to Germany, India, Thailand, Hong Kong, Los Angeles, and Chicago. I took what proved to be an ideal travel wardrobe. The same few clothes were fine for cold weather and hot, big cities and beaches. It all went into one carry-on garment bag and one carry-on underseat case. I even had room to add a few things I picked up en route.

Because what I took worked so well, I would recommend something like this to anybody for almost any trip.

> 1 lightweight black gabardine suit
> 1 navy blue blazer
> 1 gray worsted flannel trousers
> 1 blue jeans
> 2 white broadcloth shirts, plain collar
> 1 white oxford-cloth shirt, button-down collar
> 1 white cotton knit polo shirt
> 1 black-and-gray striped polo shirt
> 1 gray cashmere V-neck sweater, long sleeved
> 1 black-white-and-gray patterned silk tie
> 1 solid maroon silk tie
> 1 black silk evening bow tie
> 5 pairs black socks in silk, wool, and cotton
> 1 lightweight silk bathrobe
> 1 black nylon racing trunks
> 1 tan poplin raincoat with detachable lining
> 1 pair black plain oxford shoes
> 1 pair black slip-on loafers

The black gabardine suit worked in the daytime as a business suit, worn with a white broadcloth or oxford-cloth shirt and the black-and-white or maroon tie. In the evening, worn with the white broadcloth shirt and the silk bow tie, it served as a formal dinner suit. The jacket also went with the gray flannel trousers for less formal daytime business attire.

The blazer was invaluable—with the gray flannel trousers it served for business meetings and evening parties, and with blue jeans, for casual occasions.

The ideal travel wardrobe includes interchangeable trousers, jackets, shirts.

The rest is self-explanatory. You might want to substitute pajamas for the bathrobe (I don't like to wear pajamas) or take different ties. Don't stuff the raincoat into your luggage; carry or wear it on the plane.

How to Carry It

Good-looking and well-made luggage is more important than it might first seem. Whether you travel constantly or very seldom, get the handsomest you can reasonably afford. For most trips, an underseat bag and a garment bag are all you need. A good leather garment bag costs more than cheap vinyl, but looks better and long outlasts it. Like it or not, there is a fairly advanced snobbery in the minds of those who deal with the traveling public. Wherever you are, and whatever you're trying to accomplish, you will get more rapid and solicitous service when you carry a fine, polished leather bag than you will with the bargain-basement variety. You needn't spend a fortune, but do get something that's worth the money and doesn't fall apart quickly.

Probably the best is very plain brown leather, with good hardware and no gimmicks. The costliest, most beautiful examples can be found at Hermès in Paris, New York, and Chicago; and at Mark Cross or T. Anthony in New York.

To spend less money on luggage with more flash, you might look into the fashionable "status" ones. Louis Vuitton from Paris, sold in America through Saks Fifth Avenue stores, is instantly recognizable—dark brown vinyl-impregnated canvas with a pebbly texture, stamped all over with interlocking LV's and fleurons in yellow ochre, trimmed in saddle-tan leather. Gucci makes a wide assortment of styles using many combinations of leather, webbing, and plain or patterned canvas; hallmarks, though, are the use of red-and-green webbing, a dark grayish-brown leather, and tan canvas together with gilt buckle closing. In the United States it's sold only at Gucci stores in New York, Chicago, Palm Beach, and Beverly Hills. The other big fashion name in Italian luggage is Fendi. It's invariably of ochre-and-dark-brown fabric woven with a pattern of interlocking F's, trimmed in dark brown leather. This is sold at Henri Bendel and Bloomingdale's in New York. People are often surprised to learn how little these bags cost, considering their snob appeal.

Like many people in the fashion business, I use luggage from a "status" source. Mine is all from Fendi (at least it's marked with my own initial). A couple of years ago I was on a flight from Milan to New York organized by the Italian Trade Commission to show Italian fashions to the American public. The airplane was a chartered 400-seat jumbo jet, filled to capacity with fashion people, and when it landed and I went to pick up my Fendi luggage, I was amazed to see that there were over seven hundred suitcases made by Louis Vuitton, Gucci, and Fendi at the baggage claim. There wasn't one suitcase of another type. It was chaos for passengers to find their luggage. It took hours to sort it all out.

Maybe you don't want somebody else's initials all over the things you carry. Or don't want something so conspicuous. I have friends who swear that because so many of the supersonic set carry them, Vuitton bags tend to inspire customs officers to make a complete search. Carrying a bag with an ostentatious connotation may be a little like the red flag in the bullring.

Many men who could afford the most expensive luggage in the world carry simple, good-looking, and moderately priced molded fiberglass and vinyl luggage from one of the big American companies such as Samsonite or American Tourister. It's indestructable and has a no-nonsense look. I think the dark gray that doesn't try to imitate leather looks best.

How Much Luggage?

The number of bags you carry depends on how you travel, of course. I travel, as I expect everybody does, by plane or by car almost exclusively. Here's what I find useful for any kind of trip:

1 fold-over garment bag with straps so you can carry it like a suitcase. It needn't be leather, but it should be sturdy and waterproof.
1 underseat carry-on bag. Most airline regulations specify that this must have a combined total of no more than 44 inches. To check, add length, breadth, and width. I would again sug-

gest it be of something waterproof. If it has a shoulder strap, so much the better.

Those two do it for most travel. Other useful items for various kinds of travel are these:

1 rigid suitcase of large size, up to 25 or 26 inches wide. You can live out of this almost indefinitely.

1 overnight or weekend bag, shaped like a doctor's satchel, collapsible and soft. About 10 by 15 by 21 inches is a roomy but handy size. A shoulder strap is convenient. Some people like a duffel bag. I usually find that the thing I need is always at the bottom of a duffel, and I have to root for it. With an oblong, zipper-top bag, it's easy to retrieve a single item without unpacking the whole thing. This can be made of canvas or anything that you needn't worry about taking to the beach or the country.

1 collapsible nylon case (about the size of a briefcase, but deeper) that folds flat. This takes almost no room and adds almost no weight when packed inside a larger case. But it can be taken out later and used to hold presents, clothes, whatever you pick up along the way.

Protecting Your Investment in Luggage

· Leather luggage is often sold with protective flannel covering bags. Keep these slipcovers and use them. If you don't have a cloth bag handy when storing suitcases, throw a sheet of newspaper over them to protect from dust. Don't use plastic bags, though. Leather needs cool circulating air in order to "breathe," and while plastic keeps the dust off, it hurts rather than helps in all other ways.

· Gain room in the closet by storing smaller bags inside larger ones.

· If closet space is too tight to accommodate suitcases, the cool basement is a better place than the hot attic. Hot, dry air is hard on leather. Protect leather from basement dampness by storing off the floor. If no shelf or chair is available, get the luggage off the damp floor by piling it on a rubber-coated metal rack. The kind sold in the dime store as kitchen storage racks are cheap and perfectly suited for this.

· Before putting leather luggage away after a trip, give it a dusting and a very thin coat of neutral shoe polish. Buff now, or later for interim protection.

· If old leather has darkened at the handles, you can lighten it this way: Squeeze a lemon into a pint of cool water. Sponge on the solution and let dry. Rub well with a soft, clean cloth.

· Scuffs in leather can be concealed by coating them with paste shoe polish to match the leather. Buff, then seal with a light coat of clear shellac.

· Dirty canvas bags are best cleaned with dry soapsuds. Brush cleanser on with a damp sponge. Use wide, straight strokes from top to bottom of the bag, rinsing as you proceed with another sponge dipped in clear, cool water. Allow to dry, then go over the bag again with a clean, damp sponge if necessary.

· Zap metal handles and closures with a little Jubilee paste wax to clean, brighten, and protect them from darkening and rust.

· A bar of soap that matches your after-shave can keep a suitcase from smelling musty if you drop it, unwrapped, into the empty case before putting it away. The soap won't hurt the lining, and it will give a clean aroma to everything you pack.

13

What to Know Before You Go

50 Important Things I Have Learned About Travel

I log about 200,000 miles on planes each year and do a hell of a lot of ground travel as well. Things in the following list have all been learned the hard way for me. I pass them on, hoping they'll make your own travels a little easier.

1. Before you go, see the dentist. Have him take care of anything that's chipped, loose, or potentially troublesome. Ask for a cleaning, too. Might as well have a bright smile when you get there.

2. See your doctor for an extra prescription for any medication you usually take. Ask, too, that he recommend a general antibiotic, a pain killer, an antidiarrhea product, something for seasickness or motion sickness, and a tranquilizer or sleeping pills if you need them.

3. If you wear glasses or contact lenses, have your doctor write you an extra prescription and keep it in your wallet against the possibility of losing or breaking your glasses en route. It is always wise to travel with an extra pair of prescription glasses.

4. Have the pharmacist, in filling your prescriptions, label them all very clearly as to contents. You wouldn't want a customs inspector to consider you a drug smuggler, and in some countries that is almost a standard operating assumption. For the same reason, keep medications in the original, labeled container whenever possible, rather than transferring them to travel containers.

5. The medical profession is a worldwide fraternity. Before you leave, see if your doctor can give you a list of "good names" in the places you plan to visit. It can save a lot of worry and confusion if you should happen to need a doctor in a strange place.

6. Make a list of pertinent health information: medications you usually take, any allergies, your blood type, any chronic ailments or disabilities, names and addresses of your physicians at home, and keep this with you—in your wallet or in your carry-on bag.

7. Ask your doctor, before you leave, to recommend a nasal spray or a decongestant to take in the plane if you have a cold. Even if you don't, ask him anyway. You might come down with a cold before you come home, and pressurized cabin air in the plane can make for a miserable and dangerous flight.

8. Never take a trip anywhere without at least one name, address, and telephone number of a friend of a friend. And when you get there, *use* that contact. Call. People in places that lack a steady influx of out-of-town or foreign visitors are usually delighted by the idea of meeting someone they haven't seen every day for the past year. People in the capital cities are not much more blasé and may put you at the top of their lists, invite you for dinner that evening. If they do, you have an unparalleled opportunity to get to know the life of the city, of the country. You learn, in a way that would be impossible otherwise, how people live there. Even if the people you call are busy for the time of your stay, they will certainly offer tips on the telephone as to what's going on, the places and things that are of special interest and value to a visitor. You will be miles ahead of the person who relies solely on the "What's Going On" magazine in the hotel.

9. Start yawning just before the plane takes off, and keep yawning. Not only does it relax tense throat muscles, but it can spare you some ear-popping from the rapid change in pressure. You

might also chew gum. I like lemon-flavored gum; it speeds the flow of saliva so you swallow a lot—good for keeping the ears from stopping up and popping—and you don't feel so thirsty until the cabin attendant comes for drink orders.

10. Go easy on alcohol in the plane. One drink in the air is like two on the ground when you have it at 30,000 feet. That's why you see so many drunks on board and among the tourists newly arrived in Mexico City, Lima, and Denver.

11. When you shave and shower before leaving for the airport, use some Vaseline Intensive Care Lotion or some other product for dry skin. Rub it in well all over, and use some after-shave balm instead of an alcohol-based cologne. The cabin air is very dry and can make you feel itchy if you don't protect your skin as well as you would after a sunbath or a sauna.

12. Weather aloft has rules of its own. I have been freezing and terribly hot in planes. You can never tell beforehand how the plane will be this time. So dress for it. I think the best bet is a midweight blazer, flannel trousers, cotton shirt, and a tie. You might also have a lightweight V-neck sweater in your carry-on bag. If it's hot, you can take off the tie and jacket and be very comfortable. If it's cold, you can put on the sweater. Many of my friends travel in turtleneck sweaters, but I think they are too confining. If you feel warm, you can't very well pull off the sweater and go around half-naked. Besides, the tie wins you more points as a man of substance when you arrive. For the same reason, I think jeans are less advisable than dressier trousers.

13. Feet swell during plane travel. You'll almost certainly want to take your shoes off, so wear something that makes that a simple proposition. The best bet is loafers—penny, tassel, or Gucci. Lace-up wing tips are a bore to deal with, having to bend over to tie them when the person in front of you is stretched back in his seat. The only thing worse is trying to put your boots back on. In fact, boots are a bad idea to travel with; they take lots of room in a bag when you aren't wearing them, and they make feet miserable when you are on a plane. Leave them at home, unless you're going off on horseback.

14. Travel slippers are stowed in the seat pocket on some flights. Some very fastidious men pack a pair of glove-weight

leather slippers in their carry-on bags. I usually pad around in my socks. However you do it, do make it a point to get up and walk around as often as you can on the plane, especially on long flights. It seems to keep the circulation going so you don't feel heavy in the legs.

15. When you get up for a walk, go back to have a cup of water. Pressurized air dries you out, and a steady intake of fluids (other than alcohol, which is dehydrating in itself) will help you look and feel better.

16. Aisle seats are better than window seats if you plan to move around, and if you don't like a closed-in feeling. There isn't much to see from the window of a jet plane for most of the flight, anyway.

17. The bulkhead seat is a favorite of friends of mine who don't like to smoke or see a movie but do want to sleep and like to put their feet up when they fly. Because there is a solid wall to support your knees or your feet, rather than the soft back of another seat in front of you, nobody complains about your comfort.

18. Best of all—or potentially best—is an aisle seat in the center of a 747. With luck, the other three seats won't be occupied. You can raise the armrests and stretch out to sleep, or just laze around.

19. Stretch whenever you can. When you get up to go to the lavatory, stretch arms up over your head, rise up on your tiptoes, rotate your head slowly from left to right, raise shoulders into an exaggerated shrug, then slowly hunch them forward and down, back behind you, and relax. Back in your seat, brace hands on knees and slowly thrust your chest forward, arching your back. Any and all of these help prevent the stiffness that comes from sitting a long time in one position.

20. Whenever the stopover is long enough, get up and off the plane. Even if you do nothing more than walk around the tarmac for a few minutes, it helps. The crew would usually prefer that you remain in your seat. But ask. This is not the time for a stopover at the bar in the airport, though. Just a good brisk walk around, then back in plenty of time for takeoff.

21. Flight timing is a matter of personal preference, especially on a flight to Europe. I find that I am much less fatigued and

faster acclimated by taking a day flight from the United States. I then arrive in the evening, have a light supper and go to bed at the normal time for Paris, London, or wherever. Next day, I'm working completely on local time. Some people say they lose a working day with this system, but I feel lost in time for a day or two with the night flight. Yet, when I have plenty to do, I can work all day in New York, take the night flight and sleep on the plane, and arrive there in time for a late-morning meeting. But if you plan to do that, you must be able to sleep on the plane or you'll be at low ebb for a day or two.

22. One seldom mentioned plus for economy class: The meal is served all at once on a tray. In first class, you have to wait for the various courses to be served in turn. If you're in a hurry to get the meal over with so you can sleep, that's a drag.

23. First class or economy, the less you eat the better you'll feel when flying. On a plane, as in a hospital, the diversion of the meal is often more welcome than the food. Especially if you plan to sleep right after dinner, it's a good idea to call ahead to order the vegetarian meal. It's composed of light, easily digested fruit, salad, cheese, etc., and is often much better tasting than the meat courses.

24. Seats forward of the engines usually prove the quietest.

25. Seats adjacent to the wings are said to be in the most stable area of the plane. If a smooth ride is very important, request one of these seats in advance.

26. There is no "safe" part of a plane. Impact collision may be in the nose or the tail. Asphyxiation is the most common cause of air-traffic fatalities, so the seat close to the emergency exit would at first appear safest, but if fuel catches fire and the wing is ablaze, that's no help. Sit where you're most comfortable, and don't think about where you'll be safest. You're safe anywhere, if the flight is right.

27. If you want to do some work en route, you can use a cassette tape recorder—it won't interfere with air-to-ground communications. But keep it quiet for the in-air comfort of other passengers, naturally.

28. When traveling by boat, if you are concerned about possible seasickness, book a cabin on a lower deck. You save money

and are less likely to suffer seasickness because you are closer to the center of gravity.

29. Very cold ginger ale with plenty of lemon juice in it and a candy bar with peanuts are two of the tried-and-true seasickness remedies.

30. An external seasickness cure is to wear very loose clothes. This is no time for belt-tightening.

31. If you travel to a high-altitude city, such as Denver or Mexico City, go slow when you get there. Do everything at a leisurely pace until your body acclimates to the rarefied atmosphere. If you smoke at all, smoke less. Heart and lungs are under more strain because less oxygen is available.

32. The more you consolidate in packing and traveling, the less you lose (both in time and in stray socks). Use plastic Baggies in order to group clothes together in such categories as socks, underwear, sweaters, etc. This makes finding and keeping track of them easier as you pack, unpack, and repack. You save time, too, since most things can be quickly put into bureau drawers without removing them from the plastic bag.

33. Shoes should go in shoe bags or plastic bags before you pack them. First, stuff the shoe with socks or underwear. This keeps the shoe in shape almost as effectively as a shoe tree would. It also saves luggage space.

34. Use crumpled newspaper to stand in for shoe trees when traveling. Stuff the shoes with the morning paper when you take them off at night.

35. Especially when you carry a soft-sided bag, fill empty spaces in the suitcase with crumpled tissue paper or even newspaper wads (these should be covered over with plastic bags, though, to keep newsprint from getting on your clothes). It will keep clothes from shifting, settling, and wrinkling.

36. Pack suits in their dry-cleaner's plastic or paper coverings. This provides a certain safeguard against crushing and wrinkling.

37. Don't cram bags to the point of bursting. If you have to sit on a suitcase to close it, you've packed it too full. You damage both luggage and clothes that way. It's better even to take the overflow in a paper shopping bag than to have the case break apart from overstuffing.

38. When packing a jacket on a hanger, don't button it, but overlap the left side far over the right, and it will arrive in a less wrinkled state. If you don't take a hanger, turn the jacket shoulders inside out and fold the jacket lengthwise. Hang trousers, roll them (especially jeans and such), or drape them across the widest part of the suitcase so the fold for packing comes well below the knee.

39. Two small plastic clothespins (often found in the travel packs sold in the notions department of stores), or even two large paper clips, can be fastened onto trousers just below the hanger's crossbar. This keeps them steady and prevents their slipping down to the bottom of a garment bag.

40. Don't close your bag until the last minute, even if you pack it the night before you go. The more time the suitcase is closed, the more likely clothes are to wrinkle.

41. If you transfer shampoo or whatever to plastic squeeze bottles, it helps to squeeze the plastic container slightly after filling. Continue squeezing as you replace the cap, then release. This creates a vacuum suction that forestalls leaks.

42. Put a paper towel in the bottom of your shaving kit. Even in a plastic-lined kit, moisture accumulates, and a paper towel or terry washcloth blots it up.

43. If you use a safety razor, pack it in a small plastic bag or its own case, or just wrap the head in tissue paper. You can get a nasty cut if you reach into the shaving kit for your deodorant and find the razor blade instead.

44. If the valet service is closed when you arrive, and a suit needs pressing, you might try this to revive it: Shake out and hang in the bathroom. Turn on the hot water in the tub. Dampen a towel in hot water, and drape it over the suit. Close the tap. Shut the door of the bathroom for half an hour or so, and hope the humidity works to smooth out the creases. It often does.

45. If you buy something new for a trip, wear it a few times before you pack it. Don't plan to break in anything, especially shoes, when traveling. If you wear it now, you'll know it's comfortable, looks and feels good. Nothing that doesn't meet those criteria should go along on a trip.

46. When luggage space is tight, consider this tip I learned from Bill Fine, president of Francis Denney, Inc. When Bill needs a robe to look presentable for chambermaids and room service but hasn't room to pack a separate robe, he uses the camel fleece removable liner of his Burberry trenchcoat to stand in for one. It works perfectly as a robe, even has pockets.

47. Before you leave the country, record and declare with customs officials the serial number of your watch, your camera, and any other valuables. It can be a great help when you return. Often the customs official is unwilling to believe that your Swiss watch wasn't bought on this trip, or that you took the Nikon with you when you went to Japan, and may want to have proof-of-purchase before letting you go through customs.

48. Record, as you would your traveler's checks, the number and issue date of your passport. And, as with traveler's checks, keep this information in a separate place. If your passport is lost or stolen, it can save a good deal of time if you know the number.

49. Never leave the country without a very small phrase book (Berlitz makes the best) that fits into the pocket of your shirt or jeans or whatever you wear when you are at ease. You'll be much more at ease in a foreign country if you can ask what time the show begins or how far it is to the beach. A phrase book will tell you how. A dictionary gives you the words, but doesn't show you how to string them together in another language. I can't recommend strongly enough, too, that you spend all the time you can, before going, in seeing films from that country, listening to records of their popular songs, buying copies of their newspapers and magazines, anything that will prepare you for the startling experience of having to deal in their tongue when you're on their turf. The people in the hotel will probably speak English, but the cab driver might not. Besides, you'll enjoy it more—and so will they— if you make the effort to say things their way.

50. Tip *your* way, though. Don't hassle about trying to convert dollars into francs *plus* figuring out what's appropriate. The service is included most often. Fine. But leave 10 or 15 percent extra anyway. Tip the hotel captain, the bellboy, whoever, just as you would in America. It doesn't turn you into an Ugly American. It

may get you some very welcome extra attention, though. Adjustment to foreign currency is stress enough, without trying to pinch *pfennigs.*

Other Cities, Other Styles

Here are some quick impressions and tips on looking right and feeling at home in major cities around the world.

New York. To me, it's the capital of the world. Whatever you can't find in New York doesn't exist—because New York has everything. Everything either begins in New York or comes there immediately for certification. Style is prized in all clothes. You can wear classic Brooks Brothers or the newest fashion from Europe, but never hayseed style, such as leisure suits or white patent loafers. Dark color and conservative style is best for the daytime; at night, New Yorkers are more casual. You can't go wrong with your navy suit in the day and your navy blazer at night.

Montreal. A bit like New York, but more conservative in every area. Stick to dark suits.

Buenos Aires. Always a very beautiful and sophisticated city. It is as if Paris had been reconstructed and shipped to South America. The people are cosmopolitan—Spanish, Italian, German—but life is modeled after the England of Queen Victoria. Men are extremely clothes-conscious in Buenos Aires. More than any other city in the world, people here judge each other by clothes. Clothes are very formal, or very tweedy. It's cooler than most first-time visitors to South America might expect. You should have both tropical-weight clothes and something warmer, especially if you go during our summer months, which is winter there.

Rio de Janeiro. It's for a holiday. Nobody can (or cares to) work there. If you can get into the casual style of the place (which is very frenzied under the surface), it can be fun. It's casual to an extreme. You will see people in bathing suits going into stores and office buildings along the Avenida Atlantica. It's just off the beach,

to be sure, but it is one of the main streets of Rio. At night, usual wear for men at Antonio's and the other stylish restaurants is jeans or slacks and an open shirt, both well-fitted, as the Brazilians are very body-conscious. Besides, it's always warm, so a jacket is just a nuisance most of the time.

London. Take your raincoat. Take your umbrella, and your crepe-soled shoes. It never gets *very* cold, but it's often rainy, cool, and damp. Perhaps as a result, much of the life of London is a private, indoor life. Go to the pubs anywhere early on Sunday afternoons to see what Londoners are like when they leave home. The style, away from the financial district where very formal clothes are still worn, tends to be fairly conservative/tweedy or have very up-to-date tailoring in medium-to-light colors. People in the good hotels still appreciate it, though, if you wear a dark suit, a white shirt, and quiet tie when you go into the dining room, and conservative clothes won't get you into difficulties anywhere in London.

Paris. The French businessman is an arch-conservative, and he insists his dark, gray or navy suit be tailored to perfection. You cannot be too soberly and quietly dressed in Paris. Be sure your clothes fit well. It rains all the time there, but people never wear what they call *caoutchoucs* (our galoshes). Learn to step around the puddles and pay the very expensive taxi fares, or take some shoes that have rubber soles. Brush up on your Balzac before you go, too. Because French schools are the best and hardest in the world, the French men and women you meet tend to be more intellectual—and prouder of it—than their counterparts anywhere else. You may very well have to discuss Proust or Kafka at parties.

Amsterdam. A pleasure place, and the only city to remind me of Venice (which is, to me, the ultimate pleasure city). It's a rather formal town. When you do business, wear a dark suit. But after hours, you can be comfortable in any kind of leisure clothes. The night world in Amsterdam is incredibly organized—there are whole streets for female prostitutes, streets of gay bars, streets of drugs, etc.

Berlin. Its reputation is that nobody seems to have a concern about style, but that has changed. It is now one of the most fashion-conscious cities in the world. The most stylish, elegant clothes are appropriate for Berlin for both business and pleasure.

Munich. The youngest city I know. There are lots of schools and universities here, and all the best-looking young people from other parts of Germany come to Munich for fun. They find it in scores of nightclubs all over town. Everybody pays, though. In Munich, nightclubs, shops, everything is expensive. But you find the best, whether you're shopping for fun or clothes. It's an informal city outside of the business offices.

Vienna. Beautiful and incredibly sad in winter; beautiful and incredibly hot in summer. In winter, the museums and the restored opera are splendid. In summer, the Viennese go out to little open-air restaurants in Grinzing in the woods. They dress in a sober way at any time of year, but are very merry and always laughing, despite the fact that Vienna is the only European city to lose rather gain population.

Milan. Chicago with an Italian accent. Whatever other jokes you may have heard, it's a strong, vital city. Life is ordered and formal. Dress conservatively for Milanese businessmen. Dress pretty conservatively, too—something like a gray suit or navy blazer and flannels—when you aren't with the businessmen, and go to the Zebra or the Numero Due to dance.

Rome. My adopted city, and I love it. Life is less glamorous, less organized (and less expensive) than in Paris. It's at once a village and a world capital. It's casual—you plan an evening by running into a friend or two during a late-afternoon *passegio*, when strolling around via Condotti or on your way to Caffé Greco, or while dropping into the stores after work. (Shopping after offices close at seven o'clock is a local passion and hobby. If you don't know anybody in Rome, the place to meet them is in the boutiques after working hours.) Rome is a very casual city, but extremely conscious of style. It's definitely the place for clever color coordination. The Roman man likes to wear closely related tones of one color from head to foot. This makes him look taller and slimmer, and cuts the all-important *bella figúra*.

Athens. It's very casual, but as you might expect with lots of shipping potentates around, well-tailored. The closer you adhere to well-tailored linen suits, the more at home you'll feel. Best bet, though, is to see the unbelievable museums in and around Athens, conclude your business, and get away for a tour of the islands where you wear jeans and little else that you don't buy en route. Some great fisherman's sweaters and blue-and-white T-shirts.

Cairo. As romantic as you would expect—boats on the Nile, riding horses through the desert to see the Pyramids—and very busy. For business during the day, the lightest tropical-weight suits are best, not too dark in color. White seems completely appropriate, although cleaning is something of a problem in Egypt.

Bombay. The ideal place for seeing the very beautiful side of the lazy Indian atmosphere. Nothing lazy about the Indian movie industry, which is the most active in the world and is headquartered here. All the stars and the upper class of Bombay live seven miles outside of the city in a suburb called Juhn. The style there, and in the city, is supercasual clothes of the lightest weight.

Hong Kong. Looks like a gigantic version of Wall Street. It's another business-only city. The physical setting is lovely, but life there isn't. The going style is still very English. Wear semitropical, English-influenced things, and you'll be fine. Stay in businesslike clothes and attitude while in Hong Kong. Don't get suckered in to a lot of souvenirs, but do—if you wish—buy cameras and Japanese products at a savings. You may also find that some Hong Kong shirtmakers do a great job of copying the shirt that fits you very well, sometimes for very little money. But don't rely on them for help with style or for changing details. Usually, they're great at xerography, lousy at inventiveness. You may find the exception, but don't count on it.

Tokyo. A very difficult city, at least for a tourist who doesn't speak Japanese. It's also extremely expensive. But Japan has a real fascination, and I would never turn down the opportunity to return. In business situations, you *must* dress conservatively and look like a "serious businessman." Bring lots of business cards; you'll need all you have, because the Japanese are very quick to exchange cards with anybody they meet. Outside the business world, young men in Japan are the first to pick up new fashions and are very style-conscious.

San Francisco. You eat better here than in almost any city in the world; you dress more conservatively than in almost any city in the world. Men spend more money per capita on clothes in San Francisco than anywhere else in the United States. Unless you have some advance warning, wear your navy suit or your navy blazer and gray flannels. And bring plenty of clothes for night life, including formal attire—there are lots of black-tie dinners given.

Los Angeles. There has always been a pride of place here that emphasizes "differentness." Few people will be displeased by what you wear, whatever you wear. To offend nobody and please almost everybody, you can probably get by best in most situations with slacks and your navy blazer, give or take the tie. I have a wonderful time in Los Angeles, but can never see it as a real "city." Nobody who lives there seems to feel otherwise. At least, they don't go in for "city" clothes.

Mexico City. Tropical suits, again. Light colors and a certain degree of formality seem to look best here. The navy blazer is, as so often, a sure thing when you don't wear a suit.

Part V

FITNESS AND GROOMING

14

In All Your Worlds, It Takes More Than Clothes

Often the thirtieth birthday is a turning point in a man's life. For me, it was a time to realize responsibilities—fewer parties, more concentration on business, an awareness that spending increasing hours seated behind a desk was affecting my health and body. For you, the prod may be any milestone: starting a new job; your fifth wedding anniversary; the tenth reunion of your college class. Whatever, it can be the turning point for a better life if it causes you to take stock of the shape you're in and do something about improving it. Even if no red-letter date is at hand, and you are pleased with the way your life is going, take a minute to see how your body is weathering the trip.

Next time you shave, take a good, long look at yourself in the mirror. Check what you see against your mental image of the man you were five years ago. You don't expect (or want!) to look unchanged. But you do look for signs of a maturing progress, of healthy growth instead of decline.

Are your eyes as clear and alert as ever, or heavy-lidded and bloodshot? Skin healthy? Teeth clean and even, or tobacco-stained? If there's a full-length mirror, study the total man before you dress. Is your firm, flat stomach melting into paunch?

Be very honest, decide what needs correcting, and start doing it now! Critical self-appraisal may suggest the problem is worse than it is. In that case you'll be pleasantly surprised by how quickly you make progress, but start taking the corrective measures now.

The look of power depends on more than clothes. I think the right clothes are crucial to a happy, successful life. But this business of looking and feeling your best must take into account the body under the clothes. The best tailor in the world can't make you look good if the cloth covers a ruin. And the 10 percent of you that isn't covered—your head, your face, your hands—must look as healthy, clean, and cared-for as the rest of you.

The notion that a successful man looks drawn and exhausted from his work has been buried along with most of those who subscribed to it. In today's world the really powerful men are usually well organized and efficient enough to fit almost everything into their schedules—including the vital time needed to keep mind and body in peak condition. We expect top men to be in top shape, to be dynamic, full of vigor, glowing with the healthy color that is a by-product of good hard play.

Exercise

My own problem was too much sitting around, not enough moving around. With my doctor's okay, I signed up, right after my thirtieth birthday, at a health club. In the back of my mind was the idea that this would be too boring and require too much effort to stick with; still, I didn't want to start spreading around the middle as so many of my friends seemed to be doing. To my surprise, I felt so much better after a couple of weeks of workouts that I came to look forward to them.

What really strengthened my resolve was seeing the dramatic change in a man who joined the gym at the same time I did. He was forty-five and had really let himself go to seed. Not really obese, but twenty pounds overweight by his doctor's standard, and really flabby by anyone's standard. He came in three times a week for a calisthenics class and a little light weightlifting, followed by a swim. Men tend to get really outgoing in the gym, I found, and this fellow told me he was also cutting back on the booze-and-beef intake as well as putting in a few minutes of jogging every morning before work. After a month and a half of this, he was almost unrecognizable. It wasn't just that he had lost eighteen pounds, but he'd also lost the dragging, hang-dog look he'd previously had. Now he really struts around the gym, with that alert, confident stride that always goes along with the power look.

Exercise is a dreary word, and everybody hates the sound of it. Nobody, though, dislikes movement and getting things accomplished. Think of your program as a series of good moves, accomplishing good things for you in ways you enjoy. Physiotherapists and others who concern themselves with the body and mind have found body movements you enjoy, whatever they are, to be more beneficial than those you hate doing, no matter how efficient they are as exercise. Swimming is always billed as the best exercise. It moves and uses every part of the body in the correct bilateral way, it's refreshing, and so on. But Olympic swimming champion John Nabor has been quoted as saying "Swimming can be a pretty boring sport." If you agree, don't go near the water. Pump iron or do push-ups if you like, but only if you like. Most people don't. Then take up riding, fencing, bicycling, skating—whatever appeals to you. Many men really enjoy staying in great shape through jazz dance classes. Gardening can provide a real physical workout as well as the satisfaction of seeing (or eating) the results of your labor. The point is, you won't stick with it unless you enjoy it.

Your head should feel good while you do it; your body should feel good afterward. Next-day stiffness and sore muscles aren't the sign of a good workout but a bad one. They mean you've done too much, too quickly, after too long. Take it easy and build up to the marathon. We all know it's the weekend athlete, pushing himself too hard to make up for lost time, who gets strained muscles and worse.

Discuss projected moves with your doctor. Tell him what appeals to you, and get his suggestions as to suitability for you. Yoga, for example, is great for some back problems; for other back conditions, certain yoga moves can make things worse. Only your doctor can judge how much activity and what kind will be most beneficial in your specific case. He can alert you to your particular weak spots and needs. Probably he will give you a clean bill of health and applaud your decision to get moving in any and all directions. But do ask.

Avoid the major pitfall. That is, the excuse for not exercising. The first workout is not the hardest. It's the fourth, or the fifteenth. Whether it's going to the gym or starting tennis lessons, you begin a program with enthusiasm and commitment. But in a few weeks, it's easy to allow something to prevent you from hitting the gym or the tennis court. Just this once. It always seems a valid excuse at the time. But it breaks the thread of continuity that is vital for an ongoing commitment. Skipping today and promising yourself to make it up later establishes a nagging sense of guilt, then a resentment of the program you weren't disciplined enough to adhere to. The way around this trap is to *set realistic goals*.

Ideally, you should get some kind of physical exercise at least three times a week. You should put your body through its paces and stretch every muscle in a good workout one day, then allow the body a day of rest and recovery, then another good workout, and so on in alternation through the week. That's ideal.

But suppose you just can't find time for an hour or so of exercise every other day? Maybe your home and office schedule is so tight that one session per week seems the most you can set aside for a fitness program. Then plan on only one session a week, and be firm about it. And put your spare minutes during the rest of the week to work. Do stretching exercises in the shower, stand rather than sit when you can, take a brisk walk or a jog before dinner, do some unobtrusive isometrics while interviewing a summer job applicant or watching television—anything that keeps your body in action during those intervals when you would otherwise just sit.

Within a month, even with only one programmed weekly tone-up, I'm willing to bet you'll look and feel so much better that you will discover the extra time needed for two workouts a week, or even three.

You don't need a gym. It isn't even necessary to "suit out."

The whole beneficial process—stirring up the circulation, improving the flow of oxygen so the heart works more easily, toning and relaxing muscles, clearing the brain—can be inaugurated simply by standing up right now.

Plant your feet comfortably apart, firmly on the floor. Let your arms hang loosely at your sides. Relax your body. Bend your knees slightly. Exhale, and let your body go almost limp. Now take a slow, deep breath as you raise your hands and arms slowly out in front of you. Raise them up as high as you can, straight up over your head. Stretch your body. Pull up from the hips as far as you can, as if trying to touch the ceiling. Now roll your arms out and behind you until they are again hanging at your sides. Exhale slowly as you do this.

If there is a mirror handy, study your reflection in it. What you should see is perfect posture. Head erect, as if a string attached to the very top were pulling you up. Chest lifted up from your ribcage. Shoulders back and down. This is the position the human body likes. Everything in your body works more comfortably and efficiently when you carry yourself in this way. If you noticed a faint tingling sensation on completing the moves, it's caused by oxygen-rich fresh blood coursing through your body from brain to toes and back. If you look a little taller and trimmer, that's an extra bonus.

By making a slight mental effort to re-create this correct stance over the next few days, erect posture will gradually become habitual and unconscious. You will look more fit and energetic even standing still.

Standing correctly will help you to breathe correctly, too. Many of the health problems we face are caused, directly or indirectly, by shallow, improper breathing. Deep, cleansing breaths are vital for efficient exercise, of course. But deep, even breathing is also important for relieving tension. Next time you find yourself in a stress situation, instead of pouring a drink or popping a tranquilizer, try this one-minute breathing exercise, adapted from a technique used in the Silva Mind Control classes. Take a deep breath, and as you exhale slowly, visualize the number 3, and repeat it to yourself three times. Take another deep breath, and as you exhale, visualize the number 2, and repeat it three times. Another deep breath, exhale while visualizing and repeating the number 1 three times. Breathe normally and count down from 25 to 0.

Another technique, this one a kind of cleansing breath used in yoga, also alleviates tension. But for this you should be alone. Take a big, deep breath. Really fill your lungs, then exhale with an explosive "Hah!" Repeat a couple of times.

The right exercise program will relax tension, protect your heart, make you feel more alert, slow the visible aging process, firm your body, help you sleep, and improve your sex life. What is the right program? It depends on dozens of factors in your body, and on what you want. The way to find out what's ideal is to get a checkup that includes stress testing. Your personal physician or the company doctor may be able to do this in the office or set it up at a local hospital. A stress test measures heart rhythms, blood pressure, respiratory rate, and blood lipids (fats) before, during, and after exercise. You can be given a tailor-made regimen prescribed according to your individual needs. Next step is up to you —follow it.

Physicians and even many major corporations (Xerox, Mobil, and Exxon, for example, have set up physical training programs for employees) are primarily interested in *aerobic* exercises which benefit the cardiovascular system. The word derives from the Greek, "air-life," and a better life through better use of air is the idea. Bicycling, jogging, rope-skipping, swimming, and walking are aerobic exercises. All aerobic exercises, when done with a certain speed and rhythm for a sufficient period, increase breath and heart rates, relax and contract the muscles, and raise the body temperature and induce sweating. The pulse and heart rates become lower, and blood pressure and levels of fats in the blood drop when the body is at rest after exercise. The lower the pulse rate when you are at rest, the American Heart Association says, the healthier you are. And the normal range for an adult is between 50 and 100 beats per minute. It depends on your emotional state and your own chemistry; your healthy pulse rate might now be close to 90, but proper exercise can lower it.

EXERCISE FOR WEIGHT LOSS

What about exercising to lose weight? Don't count on it too much. The simplest way to lose weight is to cut calorie intake. In order to lose a pound of body fat you must burn 3,500 calories. Burning them up goes on all the time. Just sitting in a chair, you are burning 1.3 calories a minute. Get up for a brisk walk and you burn calories at the rate of 6 per minute. Jog and you up the rate to 10 or 12 calories per minute. So, five hours of quick jogging should burn up a pound of unwanted flesh. But remember, that's presuming you aren't adding more calories to the store that's being burned up by jogging. A marathon swimmer may lose more than twenty pounds in one grueling swim, as Diana Nyad sometimes does. But for most of us, exercise sessions alternate with meals. Dr. Jean Mayer, president of Tufts University and one of the world's leading nutritionists, has found that exercise does tend to suppress appetite to some degree. If you are trying to lose weight, schedule a quick exercise session shortly before meals; it may help you feel less hungry at the table.

If you do plan to cut back your calorie intake, don't go on crash diets or weird fad diets. Just eat less of everything. If you limit alcohol, red meat, animal fats, and sugar and other carbohydrates, you're ahead of the game. You get the same protein in three ounces of broiled chicken that you get in three ounces of hamburger, but the hamburger is so much higher in calories (not to speak of saturated fat) that you must jog an extra six or seven minutes to burn it away.

Especially if you're over, say, twenty-five and planning to lose weight, you definitely should couple your diet program with an exercise program. Because skin becomes less resilient as we grow older, a rapid weight loss without muscle-toning to accompany it can lead to a flabby, saggy body and stretch marks in the skin. If that happens, you'll look thinner, but older and more haggard.

TEN POINTS ABOUT EXERCISE

1. Do try to schedule three or four sessions of twenty to thirty minutes of exercise each week, preferably on alternate days. Physi-

ologists have found that there is no advantage in strenuous daily workouts. They have also noted that the benefits of exercise begin to reverse themselves if more than two days of inactivity follow an exercise session.

2. Don't exercise after meals. Give yourself at least two hours for digestion after a big meal. Runners believe the best way to run is with empty stomach and empty bowels.

3. Get in a session of warm-up exercises or a brisk walk just before dinner if you want to curb your appetite.

4. Choose your space and your surface carefully. Indoors or out, exercise should be done on a slightly resilient surface (grass, an exercise mat, or a carpet). Never jog on concrete if it is at all possible to jog on grass, a cinder track, or dirt. When jogging or skipping rope, always wear good running shoes with cushioned soles.

5. Don't take salt tablets (except on a doctor's advice) no matter how much you sweat. They irritate the stomach lining and can make you feel nauseated. Most people, even athletes, get from five to twenty times the salt required by the body just by salting their food. Sprinkle more liberally after perspiring heavily, and you'll be fine. Too much salt, by the way, increases fluid retention in the body and may contribute to hypertension (high blood pressure), so it's not good to overdo. You need only up to a gram of sodium daily, and three ounces of whole wheat bread alone supplies that.

6. Warm up your body with a series of limbering, relaxing, and stretching exercises before you begin a strenuous session of exercise; as a matter of fact, some limbering moves are a good idea before you begin the day, and at intervals throughout it to keep the mind alert and the body relaxed.

7. Don't, especially in winter, exercise at top speed and then stop abruptly. Taper down and allow a cool-off period for your heated body.

8. Try for a slow, rhythmic, constant pace in your movements. You can keep it up longer and produce better conditioning results. Set up a silent count in your head, or better, exercise to music.

9. Wear as much or as little as you feel comfortable in. What-

ever you wear should be loose enough for free movement, absorbent, and clean. Not only are twice-worn sweat socks bad for the health of your feet, they're an insult to those around you. Cover up in something when you take your superheated body out of the exercise room and into the cooler air.

10. Don't overdo the huffing-and-puffing to show how hard you're going about it. Hyperventilation doesn't increase the benefits of exercise; it is actually bad for you. Breathe as normally as you can, exhaling through the mouth, inhaling through the nose. Breathe in on the upswing, exhale on the downward movement. Thus you take air into your lungs when they are in position to expand, utilizing the natural bellows action.

Hair

This is the one area of his looks that every man cares about. American men spend well over $120 million a year for hair-care products, according to the Barbers, Beauticians, and Allied Industries Association. Nobody will even guess at the amount spent on haircuts, treatments of various kinds to condition, color, curl, straighten, and save the hair of the American male.

Almost any investment in your hair care is a good one. The healthy head of well-cut hair is a major sex and status symbol in our society. You can get even better returns on your investment, maybe even help preserve your hair, if you do a few things differently.

Take shampooing. It can be the best or the worst thing done to a man's hair. Unless you live in a pollution-free utopia, you should probably wash it every day. If your hair is dark or curly, it is more porous than straight fair hair and should definitely be washed daily. This won't, as some men still believe, cause hair loss. By keeping the hair and scalp clean and the scalp lightly stimulated, daily washing may actually prevent hair loss. Hair that has come out during a shampoo is dead hair, ready to fall out to make way for new growth, as dead leaves drop from a plant. A loss of about sixty hairs per day is normal. If loss seems excessive, you should comb your hair and count the strands left in your comb. It sounds silly, but it's about the only way to know whether your

hair is really going or you are just worrying too much over a normal state of things.

Here's the best way to shampoo: Rinse hair in the shower
with plenty of lukewarm water to flush away surface dirt. Pour a
little shampoo (about the size of a half-dollar coin should be
adequate) into your wet palm. Rub palms together to work up a
lather. Don't pour shampoo directly onto the hair, but work up
lather first, then put it on. With fingertips, lightly spread the lather
evenly over your head, massage lightly and briskly with the fingertips into the scalp, and work the lather out to the ends of the hair.

Rinse several times under plenty of lukewarm water. If you
shampoo every day, you should ignore directions to lather, rinse,
and repeat. One lathering will do it unless your hair is very oily or
very dirty. You might want to rinse more often, though. Be sure
all the shampoo is out. Rinse with the coldest water you can stand.
Now, either apply a conditioning rinse, letting it stay on long
enough to do its job and then rinsing it out, or go to the towels.

Blot your hair dry with the towel. Don't rub it. Hair is very
elastic when it's wet, and rubbing to dry can snap the hair shaft.
Blot well, just pressing the towel to your wet head. Then use
your fingertips to lift the hair so it dries quickly in the air. In a
few minutes, when hair is damp but no longer wet, you can use a
blow dryer/styler, a heat lamp, your fingers, or a wide-tooth comb
to dry it and put it in place. Never use a brush on hair that is even
slightly damp. This tugs at hair and can break it.

SAVING TIME, HAIR, AND MONEY: THE RIGHT SHAMPOO

If you wash your hair daily, you needn't worry about a special
shampoo for dry or oily hair, and you needn't worry about pH
balance. The thing to get is a mild shampoo, one that is gentle
in cleansing, such as those formulated for babies. The special
formula shampoos are made to work in such a way that they will
overcorrect the problem when used on a daily basis. Especially
when used full-strength and according to the usual directions to
lather twice.

Here's the time-and-money saver: *Whatever shampoo you use,
cut it in half.* When you buy shampoo, pour half of it out into
another clean bottle or jar. Add an equal amount of plain, cool

water to the shampoo, so as to dilute it 50 percent with water. Shake well to mix. Save the other half of the bottle for later use, or dilute it now and keep it at your gym or club or wherever else you need it.

You save time whenever you shampoo with this diluted cleanser, because you can do a thorough job of rinsing in far less time. Thorough rinsing is important, because unless *all* the shampoo goes, hair doesn't shine as it should; you can even develop a case of pseudo-dandruff from the flaking crust of dried-on shampoo that adheres to the scalp. And you help your hair by using a thinner washing medium. It lathers easily and spreads through the hair and over the scalp with less manipulation of the fragile wet hair. The saving in money of such a two-for-the-price-of-one deal is obvious.

CONDITIONING

The purpose of a conditioner is to coat the hair shaft with a protective, transparent layer (usually containing molecules of protein). The hair does *not* absorb this protein into the hair shaft. But the protein layer does cling to the outside of the shaft, filling in any microscopic pits or breaks, and protecting it, much as a silicone coating protects your raincoat. The conditioner is a good idea if your hair gets rough treatment in the sun or the wind, if you use heat lamps or blow dryers on it, if it is very fine or brittle, and certainly if you color or otherwise chemically treat it. The best person to ask about the choice and use of a conditioner for your particular hair is the person who cuts it.

DRYING WITH ELECTRICAL EQUIPMENT

Most men wear much shorter hair than was the case a few years ago, and you may find your hair doesn't need any help from electrical equipment for styling and drying when it's worn short. So much the healthier; hot-air drying can be damaging to the hair unless properly done. To watch the proper way in action, study what your haircutter does. You probably won't be able to duplicate his styling feats exactly, but you'll have a head start. Ask him to explain or show you the best way. In general, these are the things to remember with a dryer:

· Hair should be only damp, not wet, when you begin.

· Hold the dryer at least six inches away from your hair and *keep it moving.* You can overheat hair by aiming a steady blast at it. Wave the dryer from side to side.

· Dry one section at a time. That is, dry hair in back of your head first, then dry the left side, the right side, and finally the front. Use your fingers to lift and separate hair as you dry it.

· When hair is almost completely dry, switch the dryer setting to "style" and use a brush to make hair do what you want, according to what your stylist has shown you. Best kind of brush to use is one with nylon bristles with rounded tips set into a flexible rubber pad.

If it all sounds like a lot of trouble, frankly, it is. Have your hair cut in a way that doesn't require a lot of fooling around with brushes and dryers to maintain good looks. Never try to change the normal growth pattern of your hair by complicated maneuvers with equipment. The result is never as long-lasting (or as good-looking) as giving your hair its head.

AS THE HAIR IS CUT

Your hair grows about half an inch each month. For it to look its best at all times, you should have it cut twelve times a year. That's twelve chances annually at an immediate and big improvement in the way you look to the world and feel about yourself. You always feel like a new man after a good haircut, but a bad one takes much longer than a month to outgrow. You owe it to yourself to go to the best man you can possibly afford for your monthly cut.

You and he have to work out what to do. It depends so much on the shape of your head, your body, your life, that there can't be any real tips to pass along. There is one thing that you should consider, I think: *Wear the kind of hair style that accords with the style of clothes you wear.* If you are consistent, honest, and authentic in your life, that should be no problem. If you are dishonest with yourself and others about who you are, your hair will give you away. The fellow who aims for an antiestablishment look with lots of unkempt hair in his world of leisure will always look wrong, never authentic in the world of business if he works at an establishment kind of job. Decide what your style really is, then shape your hair to it.

SOME SPECIAL CONSIDERATIONS AND PROBLEMS

Dandruff. In a very mild form, with a slight itching of the scalp and a few random flakes, dandruff is very common and can usually be controlled by regular washing of the scalp and hair (being careful not to aggravate a dry scalp condition). But severe dandruff, called seborrheic dermatitis, is another matter. Then the scalp itches severely and can become inflamed, and the hair is filled with flakes. Don't attempt to treat this yourself, but go to a dermatologist or physician. Medicated prescription products can help. In some mild cases, though, it's only a pseudo-dandruff that produces white flakes. These may be from hair spray or shampoo that has not been properly removed.

Baldness. More than half of all men are affected by baldness by the time they are sixty-five. More than 10 percent of all men start losing their hair at age twenty-five due to MPB (Male Pattern Baldness). This is genetic and, contrary to what you may have heard, can derive from the maternal or the paternal side, according to the American Medical Association. So neither your mother's father's full head of hair nor your father's will guarantee that you will keep your hair. The male hormone androgen does cause the genetic predisposition to manifest itself, though, so there may be a real basis for the idea that bald men are more virile. Because of the growth pattern of hair, some hair loss is natural and nothing to worry about. Hair grows for as long as two years. Then an individual hair rests for several months. A new hair forms below it in the follicle, and pushes out the old, dead hair. Hair that is resting, waiting to be shed, drops easily. If you think you are shedding more than sixty to seventy-five hairs a day, that's the time to consider talking it over with your doctor. Some hair loss is temporary, as after an illness, but MPB is not. There are no known methods to arrest MPB, and no "cures." There are two ways to disguise or correct it, though: hair transplants, and hairpieces or toupees.

Both are expensive, but better investments than a string of cheaper treatments and promised cures that don't work.

Hair transplants. These are expensive but permanent. The process is not especially painful, but it is slow and painstaking. Basically, it goes this way: About fifteen hair roots in a tiny circle of skin are removed from the side or the back of the scalp. A corresponding area of skin is removed from the bald part of the scalp, and the "plug" with hair is inserted. This may be stitched or taped in place, or simply covered with a nonstick dressing. About twenty of these transplants can be done in a single session, but to cover a scalp that is almost completely bald, upward of three hundred grafts may be needed. Not only is it necessary to schedule the transplant sessions a few days or a week apart, there is also a considerable time lag between grafting and new growth. Transplanted hair falls out within a month after grafting, and the new hair grows in at the normal rate (that is, about half an inch per month) approximately two months later. A hairpiece or toupee can be worn over the transplant area with no harm. Bear in mind that not all men are suitable candidates for hair transplantation. It depends on the kind of baldness, the area to be covered, the amount of hair remaining at the back and sides of the scalp, and the condition of your blood vessels (as they must supply the proper growing conditions for the grafts). But it has worked for Frank Sinatra, Senator William Proxmire, and thousands of other men. If you are seriously concerned by thinning hair, check your own physician or your county or state medical society for the names of qualified specialists.

Hair weaving. Weaving is extremely popular, especially with black men for whom keloidal scarring may make hair transplants less effective. Your hair is threaded through an open-weave mesh, which covers the bald spot. The hair is knotted to secure the mesh flat against the scalp; then real or artificial hair is woven through. The only disadvantage to hair weaving is the upkeep. As the hair that holds the hairpiece grows, the mesh backing moves away from the scalp, and you must go back in for a retightening each month or so. It is also more difficult to keep the scalp clean. If you are considering hair weaving, be sure to get the names of really top experts. Look in the phone book, check those names against the Better Business Bureau's files, then visit the two or three places that sound best. Look at the work each of them does, then decide on the one you like best.

Hair implants. Implants are a pretty scary way of covering baldness. A doctor inserts stitches or staples into the scalp, hair is threaded through the staples, and then the staples or stitches and the attached hair are tightened into place. Some people, many in fact, tolerate the treatment well. Some do not. For the latter, foreign bodies in the scalp produce rather violent reactions.

Hairpieces. Toupees and hairpieces are the quick and easy way to cover baldness. But don't be too quick to buy a hairpiece. Shop very carefully, and be prepared to spend. Nothing looks worse than a cheap toupee. If you are going to do it—even after Telly Savalas, Yul Brynner, Isaac Hayes, and so many others have demonstrated that bald can be sexy today—then do it right. Look in the Yellow Pages, check out all the listed names with the Better Business Bureau, then visit the ones that sound best. Ask to see what they do, touch and compare the differences in hairpieces made with natural hair (more expensive, more realistic, but more trouble— they must be recolored every couple of months) and synthetic (less cost, less upkeep, often less good-looking); find out the differences between comfort and expected life-span of various kinds of backings (there are mesh backs, transparent lace mesh supports that glue on, and perforated rigid plastic bases, among others); ask every pertinent and impertinent question you can think of before you buy. You'll be glad you did, because it's the only way to insure the long-term satisfaction that is possible with a good hairpiece.

Coloring. Dyeing, bleaching, or coloring your hair is first, last, and always a job for the pros. Never do anything to change the color of your hair at home. Please, if you want to cover gray or lighten brown or anything else, go to the best men's salon in town and let them do it. That way, if it comes out somewhat off-color, you have recourse, and they will correct the damage. If you botch it yourself—and there are more botched jobs around, free for the staring-at, than good ones, which nobody notices—you just have to wear it for days, even weeks. If you want to cover gray and you're over thirty-five, don't match your hair to what it was at eighteen. As pigment in the hair fades, skin tone changes for the lighter, so pick (with the colorist's help) a shade several degrees lighter than you remember your hair being then. And if you do color gray hair and don't want anyone to be the wiser, start doing so before it's very gray, unless you're moving to Venezuela or someplace. Also, don't get into a bind about gray hair. It hasn't hurt Cary Grant.

Skin

The point of good skin care is, of course, to keep it clean and healthy looking. Since skin is the largest organ of the body, and accounts for about 6 percent of your total weight, keeping it in good shape is a big, important job. Generally, skin is dry, oily, or a combination of the two. How to clean it depends on the kind of skin you have. If your skin starts to shine around the nose and forehead about an hour after you wash your face, it's oily and probably tends to break out. The idea is to degrease it. You should wash your face as often as three times a day with any good soap and warm, not hot, water. You might also want to use a cleansing astringent freshener (Seba-Nil towelettes are good and convenient to use) once or twice a day.

Dry skin usually feels tight and flaky after washing, seldom looks shiny, and almost never breaks out. Go easy on the washing. You may want to rinse your face often, but don't use soap more than once a day. Don't use a "deodorant" soap to wash with; instead try a mild one, such as a castile or baby soap, or a nonsoap such as Basis. Avoid alcohol-based after-shaves and use an after-shave emulsion to soothe the skin after shaving. Get hold of a moisturizing lotion, such as Vaseline Intensive Care, and use it all over after your shower. Wash and shower with warm water, never hot and be sure you rinse really well. Soap residue will add to the discomfort of dry skin.

Combination skin is the so-called normal skin. You should wash the face twice a day with any good soap, use warm water, not hot, rinse well, and (especially in winter) use a moisturizing body rub after the shower to make you feel more comfortable.

Smoking affects your skin. Prolonged smoking over years tends to give the face a grayish cast and increases wrinkling. The only way to counteract that is to stop smoking, but taking good care of your skin will minimize the damage.

Facials and massages feel good, but most dermatologists seem to feel that a facial doesn't do the skin any long-term good. It can, in fact, damage the skin. Pulling, rubbing and tugging the delicate skin of the face eventually stretches and breaks down the tissue.

A suntan is something everybody wants, and, for long-term health and looks of the skin, no one should have. Of course, you will go out and try for a tan anyway, no matter what the doctors say. Just don't burn. Use some kind of good sunscreen cream or lotion; work up to a maximum exposure, starting with only ten minutes or so in the morning until you build up a "base," and even when you are tanned, try to stay out of the sun at noon. Rays are direct then, and ten minutes of noon sun burns you more quickly than half an hour of sun at 9:00 A.M. Ultraviolet rays cut through water, too. Don't think you aren't getting tanned—or burned—just because you're swimming rather than lying in the sun. Wear dark glasses whenever you're in the sun. Really dark glasses. They should be dark enough so that your eyes can't be seen clearly through the lenses. Don't just cover up when you suspect you've had more than your share of sun; go indoors.

If in spite of everything you do get a sunburn, here are some tips to ease the pain: Put cold, wet tea bags (the tannic acid is the active ingredient) on your eyes, or pat your face with them; cucumber slices, used as compresses on the eyes, may reduce swelling; soak a handkerchief in vinegar and lay it over the shoulders or wherever it hurts most; have a lukewarm bath, just lying still and not scrubbing, and use some body lotion afterward.

Facial and Body Hair

For a man to let his beard grow is a declaration of independence. In the past, only the master of the house could have a beard. A servant with a beard or a mustache was unthinkable. Today, you never see anything but clean-shaven employees in a really first-class hotel or restaurant. But a man who considers himself a free spirit often feels a beard or mustache makes him look stronger, more authoritative, older, sexier, hipper—the reasons are almost endless.

Think long and hard before you let it grow. Know your public. Older men and women don't, as a rule, like facial hair. Younger men and women usually do, although even they often think it's covering up a weak chin or bad skin, or that you're trying to hide some psychological problem behind the hair. A beard or mustache may reduce your credibility if you work in law, banking, or sales. If you work in a so-called creative field, it may help you in many instances. A mustache is more widely acceptable than a beard.

If you decide to do it, all you have to do, of course, is stop shaving the part you want to cover and wait. If you're going off on holiday or into the hospital or some other fairly secluded place, so much the better. You'll look like a bum for a couple of weeks before it becomes obvious that you are growing a mustache or a beard. It can be itchy there for a while, too. At the end of a month, you should have a pretty fair idea of what's going to happen. You may want to call it a day. Sometimes men find that the growth pattern is not all it might be. Facial hair can grow in all one color, in a crazy quilt of red, blond, brown, and gray, or in a solid gray or red or brown that seems to have nothing to do with the color of the hair on your scalp. But you might like the contrast. Some men do, and in New York a while ago there was even a sort of fad among some men with dark hair of bleaching out the facial hair to very pale blond.

No matter what color the facial hair is, it must be neat and simple. Leave the elaborate beard and mustache effects to the history books. They looked better on Kaiser Wilhelm and General Burnside than they will on you. Just aim for a natural growth, on the short side. Treat facial hair as you do the hair on your scalp. That is, shampoo daily, rinse very well, use a little conditioner if the beard is very dry or coarse, and comb and trim regularly, always when hair is dry. Have the barber even cut your beard or mustache when he cuts your hair. In between haircuts, keep it neat and even with a pair of short, sharp scissors to cut away straggle every few days. That last suggestion is not as easy as it sounds. It takes practice, but all beards and mustaches look better for trimming, so practice often. Here are the ways.

For a close trim: Rest the head of the comb against your cheek, with the teeth at a slight angle out from the face. Use scissors to clip off the hair that protrudes through the teeth of the comb. Go down from cheek to jaw, keeping pressure even. When you finish, comb straight down, then without the comb, trim any long hairs you missed.

For a full beard: Comb down, then just use the scissors to clip off any wild hairs or stray growth. If your hand is very steady, you may be able to use an electric razor, but the scissors are more easily controlled.

Once you have a beard or mustache, remember to be extremely neat about eating and drinking. It sounds ridiculous, I know, but I am amazed at how many men who should know how to use a napkin, walk around with crumbs and dribbles in their beards. Realize, too, that just as hair on the head absorbs and holds the odors of cigarette smoke, so does the beard or mustache. And to a much greater degree. Many women say they enjoy kissing a man with a beard. But nobody likes to get near a beard that reeks of stale cigarette smoke. If you start growing facial hair, that might be a good time to stop the bad habit.

UNWANTED HAIR

Eyebrows. Brows that grow straight across the bridge of the nose give some men a fierce, scowling appearance. If this is a problem for you, go ahead and get rid of some of the hair over your nose. It can be done rather expensively but permanently with electrolysis, or quickly and easily with plucking. I can't figure out why, but some men are uptight about others knowing they pluck a few hairs from between their eyebrows. If you are, hide the tweezers. When plucking, don't get carried away and reshape your whole eyebrow. That looks strange, and—ask any woman—it's damn hard to do well. To pluck just a few hairs over the bridge, here's how: Wash and dry the area, rub with a piece of cotton soaked in rubbing alcohol, clean the tweezers with alcohol. (It's easier to get a good hold on hair if it's dry and free of oil.) Pull up, in the direction of hair growth, tweezing only one or two hairs at a time. Finish with another quick alcohol rub.

Ears and nose. Never pluck hair growing in the nostrils or ears. This should be trimmed carefully with blunt scissors. Many older men find hair growing on the surface of the nose. This can be plucked, using the same technique as for the eyebrows. Never pluck hair growing from a mole, though. See the dermatologist if this is a problem.

Back and shoulders. Almost every man has some hair growth on his back or shoulders. If it's a stray, occasional hair—and if it bothers you—pluck it. For a heavy growth of hair that really disturbs you, ask the doctor or dermatologist about the advisability of electrolysis, or a depilatory cream or wax. Don't even consider shaving; that's a battle you'll lose to stubble.

SHAVING

There are two ways to approach shaving. Use an electric razor or a safety razor, whichever is more comfortable. If you do it right, there is no difference in results. Here's the right way for each.

With safety razor, if convenient, shave after your shower. Otherwise, wash your face, rinse off the soap, and leave face as wet as possible. Warm water softens whiskers. Splash more water on your face and then apply your shaving cream. Don't use too much, because an excess merely clogs the razor. Here's the important part: Give the shaving cream sixty seconds to soften your beard. It's enough time to apply underarm deodorant, clean your nails, or whatever else, but a shaving cream needs that minute in order to do the chemical job that makes the manual job of shaving easier. Rinse the blade under hot running water before you start shaving, then rinse again and again. Rinse after every few strokes in order to get the cleanest shave. When you finish shaving, rinse your face repeatedly (fifteen times is not too much) in warm and then cool running water to get rid of all the residue of hair and soap. Finish by smoothing in an after-shave emollient cream or alcohol-based after-shave. Which one depends on your skin. If it's dry, use a lotion or cream.

With an electric razor, the problem is to keep the whiskers standing up and bone dry. The solution is to rid them of natural oils by using an alcohol-based preshave lotion. Shave before your shower for a closer electric shave; skin won't be plumped up by moisture then. Clean the head of the razor before you start. Rather than dragging the razor across your face, try pressing it against the skin in staccato strokes, then finishing up with an overall sweeping movement. This is more effective and easier on the skin. Clean skin after shaving with a cold-water rinse or two followed by a gentle massage with a skin-soothing emollient cream or, if skin is very oily, an alcohol-based after-shave.

Eyes

Of all the energy your body expends in the course of the day, 25 percent of the work is done by the eyes. If your eyes are fatigued, you feel tired all over. Take good care of them and you'll look and feel better as well as see better.

Eyeglasses. Glasses can, if you choose them correctly, make you look even better than you do without them. Because there is now so much variety available in good-looking frames, many former contact-lens wearers have gone back to glasses. There are even some men around who wear frames fitted with plain glass; because they are very young, or look less powerful or intellectual without glasses, they wear them as an authoritative prop. Generally, darker frames are more forceful and noticeable. If your face is small, lighter frames won't look so overpowering. Consider the shape of your face when you select a frame. If it's round, get a frame with a vertical shape to slim the face; if it's long, pick a horizontal frame with flat top and bottom rims; if your nose is long, get a low bridge; if short, a high one. Whatever shape and color you choose, keep the lenses and the frames clean. Don't wipe them on a handkerchief—you'll eventually scratch the lenses. Wash them in water and mild detergent once or twice a day and dry them with a soft towel. Handle the glasses by the rim around the lenses when you put them on and take them off. Never put your glasses face-down on a table when you take them off; they'll get scratched. Fold them, and if you are a particularly tidy sort, put them away in their case. It's troublesome but wise.

Contact Lenses. Contacts are a whole new ball game. Now you can even play ball wearing contacts since the development of soft lenses, which don't pop out of place. Soft lenses are more trouble to fool with than the old-fashioned hard lenses. They require the mixing of a fresh soaking solution and overnight boiling every night. But they are undergoing constant improvement, and a no-boil lens has been developed. One major advantage to soft lenses is that they can usually be worn with comfort almost immediately. Not everybody can wear soft contacts, though. Astigmatics, because of an uneven shape of the cornea, usually cannot. Softs may also be somewhat less effective in visual correction than hard contacts or glasses. But contacts, hard or soft, can be great for a man who doesn't like wearing glasses. Now there are even bifocal contacts. Still, don't throw your glasses away. You should alternate the wearing of glasses and contacts. There is a chance that contacts can alter the shape of the cornea over the course of years, and you still need glasses for emergencies such as losing a contact lens.

Goggles. A good idea not just for welders, goggles are for every man in a situation where eye injury is possible. Wear goggles when you swim in highly chlorinated water, when you play tennis or ski, or do anything else that poses potential trouble for eyes. Some of the goggles you can get are very good-looking. Check the sporting goods stores.

Eyedrops. Use eyedrops sparingly. Especially the ones that whiten your eyes immediately. They constrict the blood vessels that make the whites of the eye red. But eventually, as these vessels work overtime to regain normal size, the eye develops varicose veins and remains permanently reddened. The eye produces its own natural washing fluids—tears, for example—and it's not a good idea to monkey around too much with mother nature. Ask your doctor to recommend a good eyedrop formula, and use it in moderation. Cold water and cotton compresses may work to relieve redness just as well as anything else you might try. If you get a particle of dust in your eye, try bathing the eye with plain cold water in an eyecup. If discomfort persists, see the doctor, or go to the emergency room of the local eye clinic or hospital.

Black Eyes. If you should ever have a black eye, don't waste a good steak to press against it. A compress of cotton soaked in ice water is the best remedy.

Teeth

Surely you know how important an attractive smile is. And you know what you have to do to keep it attractive. By now, your dentist and periodontist have told you that the old way to brush is not the best way, and you know all about plaque and how to use dental floss. If you don't, where have you been? Where you should be is in the dentist's office. If there is anything you don't like about the teeth you have, or the shape they're in, ask your dentist what can be done. You might be amazed at the strides made in corrective, restorative, and cosmetic dentistry as well as in simple preventive care. If teeth are out of line, you can wear braces—at any age. Michigan State Senator William B. Fitzgerald did, and took the floor with braces on. You needn't even be called "zipper mouth" anymore. New braces that are made of an almost invisible plastic have been developed. Specialists can correct almost every problem today. There is absolutely no reason to suffer embarrassment about the state of your teeth or, worse, to join the ranks of the 20 million Americans who have lost all their teeth. If fear of pain is holding you back, grow up: Novocain and other painkillers will alleviate most discomfort. But if it's money, check the excellent low-cost dental clinics operated by most universities. Investigate the possibility of prorated fees with your dentist, periodontist, orthodontist, or any specialist in this vital area of personal health and good looks.

Hands and Nails

We don't do much conscious thinking about hands, but the two largest areas of the cerebral cortex are set aside for control of right- and left-hand motor action, and the hands contain a quarter of all the bones in the body. In addition, hands are often one of the sources of a man's sexual appeal. You can improve the strength, dexterity, and look of your hands without much trouble. Here are a few ways.

Manicures. Manicures are an inexpensive luxury. Just be careful the manicurist doesn't put clear nail lacquer on to make your nails shiny. I wouldn't let him or her buff the nails too much, either. Glittering fingernails for men are frowned on by almost everyone.

Emery boards. Professional manicurists use emery boards to shape fingernails. Metal files tend to leave the nails more ragged, more prone to splitting and trapping dirt. If you file down your nails, file from edge to center in one direction only. Don't saw back and forth. Some authorities say that nail clippers are even better to encourage healthy nails, provided you use them regularly and trim off only a very small portion of nail each time. Whether you file or clip, go for an even, short rounded line. Don't cut too deeply into the corners—that encourages splitting, tearing, and even infection.

Cuticles. Never cut cuticles. They help protect the nail bed from infection. Lift them very gently when you wash your hands. Use an orange stick, and be very careful.

Whites of nails. These are best kept white by using an orange stick wrapped in a little wet cotton. A metal scraper will scratch the inside of the nail, allowing dirt to get trapped in the scratches. Before a really grimy job, run your fingernails over a bar of white soap. Then when you wash later, there will be no trapped grime to get rid of. And to keep hands clean, wear gloves. Cotton work gloves are more comfortable than rubber ones, which trap perspiration inside.

Keratin. This is the technical name of the protein of which nails and hair are composed. A balanced diet assures that your body produces an abundant supply, so you don't need to take calcium supplements, gelatin, or anything else for healthy nails.

Ridges. The nails can develop ridges because of poor health or simply increasing age. If these really bother you, they can be smoothed down with an emery board, but you must follow with a buffing to restore luster to the nail.

Hand Creams. Lotions and creams are a good idea for men as well as women. The skin of the hands is lacking the supply of subcutaneous oil glands that keep the rest of the body lubricated. If you aren't to have wrinkled, old-looking hands, you have to help out with some kind of moisturizing agent. Rubbing a water-soluble cream into your hands and under your nails helps keep them free of dirt and stains, too.

Calluses. File down calluses with a pumice stone or emery board, because when they go too deep, painful fluid buildup between the layers of skin may result.

Blisters. Do not pierce blisters on the hands. If the blister breaks, wash it with plain water, clean with antiseptic, and cover with a Band-Aid.

Dexterity. The dexterity of your hands can be improved with this exercise, which stretches and flexes finger and wrist muscles: Lay a sheet of paper flat on a table. Reach out with your left hand and crumple the paper into a ball. Repeat with another sheet of paper using the right hand. The bigger the paper, the more effective. Or make the same movement without paper.

Feet

They're getting bigger. According to the American Footwear Industries Association, the shoe size of the average American soldier is now approaching 10½D; at the time of the Second World War, it was 8D, and at the time of the Civil War, 7C. But apparently feet aren't getting better. An estimated 70 percent of American men suffer from foot problems of one sort or another, and few do anything about correcting them. We spend more than $11 billion on shoes in this country, but only about $107 million on foot-care products.

Take care of your feet if you expect them to hold up. If you walk seven miles a day (and just pacing the office can account for almost that much) you have subjected your feet to pressure of about 1 million pounds. Your feet reflect the total health of the body. In Japan, Dr. Yaichiro Hirasawa of Shizuoka University is responsible for a three-minute daily series of foot exercises that are mandatory for personnel of the Honda Motor Company. The movements were devised to cut fatigue for workers who must stand long hours. Dr. Hirasawa also claims 90 percent accuracy in diagnosing ailments in the body through symptoms in the feet. Pain or stiffness in the big toe means liver trouble; in the second or third toe, the stomach; fourth toe, the spleen; and little toe, the bladder.

Aside from buying and wearing well-fitting shoes and socks, and changing them regularly, you should keep your feet and leg muscles exercised and your feet clean and dry. Here are the ways.

· Walk whenever you can. It causes an increase in circulation, and helps prevent varicose veins. When possible, walk barefoot, but only on a yielding surface such as sand, grass, or carpet.
· Strengthen muscles that support the long arch by standing with feet rolled outward, bending the knees, and relaxing the feet.
· To strengthen toes, stand with one foot on an aluminum beer can. Curl the toes down over the can, trying to bend them completely around the curve. Do this ten times, eventually working up to forty or fifty. Also strengthen toes by using them to try

to pick up small objects—a dozen marbles scattered on the carpet, a pencil, or a small rubber ball.

· To stretch and loosen calf muscles, stand in bare feet facing a wall and about three feet away from it. Turn toes in, with your weight on outer edges of the feet. Place your hands against the wall, and lean against it. Keep your head up and back rigid as you bend your arms and lean your body as close in to the wall as possible or until your head touches the wall. Hold for a few seconds, then push away from the wall. Repeat five times. This is good not only for feet and legs but also for chest and arms.

· To correct pronation (a common foot ailment in which the ankles roll inward and the arch flattens), walk barefoot around the room, in as straight a line as possible, with the toes slightly curled in, weight on the outer edges of the feet.

· Dr. Alvin Kanegis, president of the New York Podiatrists' Association, says the pertinent questions he asks his patients about foot care are: "How often do you wash your hands?" and "How often do you wash your feet?" To keep feet really fit, he says, they should be washed at least twice a day. He recommends soaking the feet, drying thoroughly, massaging with a nonmedicated foot cream, then dusting off with a foot powder. When you soak your feet, you might enjoy using a special foot bath preparation that is antibacterial and smells fresh. You can have a cool, hot, or lukewarm soak. I find that a hot foot bath, using soap and water along with the soaking powder preparation, followed by a cold-water soak, has the most relaxing effect. Use a nail brush to get your feet really clean. Dry them thoroughly and you should never be troubled by athlete's foot or ringworm; follow with a massage cream or regular after-bath body lotion if you like, but don't skip using a foot powder. It helps absorb perspiration and keeps your feet dry and comfortable.

Diet

There are dozens of books that can tell you more than I could about what—and how much—you should eat. If you are concerned with losing some weight, all you have to do is cut down on the size of the portions and step up your activity. If your weight problem is more than a question of losing five or ten pounds, look into the Weight Watchers program for men. It has produced fantastic results for several people I know. It is said by the experts to be nutritionally sound and psychologically satisfying, and it seems to work.

VITAMINS AND MINERALS

Do you know any vitamin experts? It sometimes seems that every third person I meet tells me of some new discovery. They confide that if I take lots of this, that, or the other vitamin supplement, I will experience this or that miraculous change in health and well-being. Since we don't as a rule eat a wide variety of very fresh foods, but must depend on luck to get the really fresh vegetable that has all its nutrients intact, we can't depend totally on food for the vitamins we need. The best idea, though, is to take a vitamin and mineral supplement that supplies all the U.S. Recommended Daily Allowances in addition to eating as much fresh, raw, or quickly cooked vegetables, fruits, and other whole natural foods in the widest variety. If you suspect your diet and your vitamin supplement are not supplying you with enough of a specific vitamin, your best bet is to talk it over with a nutritionist or with your doctor (if he has a sympathetic attitude about vitamins; many doctors don't). Be wary of self-prescribed megadoses of any single vitamin. They can sometimes do more harm than good, because vitamins must work in a synergic relationship; that is, each vitamin seems to aid the work of another. Unless they are operating in the proper balance, vitamins don't help the body as they should. Most excess vitamins will be excreted in the urine. But not the oil-soluble vitamins, such as vitamin A. Overdoses of A can be the cause of severe liver damage. Also, never take vitamins on an empty stomach. Food is necessary not just for your health and comfort, but for your vitamin pill to work.

ALCOHOL

I like to drink—in moderation. But moderation to one person might seem like boozing it up to another. Individuals vary so much in tolerance for alcohol, and even the effects on the same person vary widely according to his state of mind and health. One thing is sure, though, alcohol destroys the B vitamin complex in the body; so if you drink, you need more vitamins. Alcohol is also high in calories that do not nourish the body but do add weight and bloat. Alcohol can be hard on the circulation and on the liver, and drinking makes you less tolerant of the hot weather and more fatigued after exertion. These are all good reasons to watch your step with liquors, wines, and spirits.

A Five-Minute Session for Total-Body Toning

I don't want to end on a negative note by saying why you shouldn't drink too much. Let me finish instead by telling you about a healthier way of feeling better for a much longer time. What follows is a quick series of good moves for your body—and your spirit. These can be done almost anywhere and anytime, and they won't carve a chunk out of your schedule at home or on the road.

Aerobics, as I said before, are the healthiest kind of good moves. You may want to do some aerobics, or you might be interested in the kind of muscle bulk that only weightlifting can give. On the other hand, you might hate the whole idea of regular exercise altogether. No matter where you fall on the fitness scheme, I think you should keep yourself limber enough to get around. If you do only the following five-minute session of stretching and relaxing once or twice a day for a couple of weeks, you'll feel and look so much better that I believe you'll want to step it up. You can also use these moves as a great way to warm up before going on to the programmed exercises that you and your doctor have determined. And they are good if you travel frequently, because you can do them in any hotel room as easily as anywhere else—no mats, weights, or equipment are needed.

Take everything slow and easy. Inhale on the upward movement, exhale on the downswing. Nothing here should prove time-consuming or difficult if you are in reasonable health, but if you have any medical complications, you may want to check even these mild exercises with your doctors.

If you are really strapped for time, you can begin and end

with the first movement. It was recommended to me by the former coach of the San Diego Chargers football team as the single best conditioner possible.

1. With feet comfortably apart, hands on hips, rise up on the balls of your feet and lightly jump in place sixty times, knees slightly apart.

2. In same starting position, lift left knee high and as close to the chest as you can, as if walking rapidly in the surf; follow with the right. Start with a count of ten, working up to twenty or thirty.

3. Stand, feet comfortably apart. Raise arms and clasp hands as high over your head as possible. Stretch and pull the torso up from the hips, as if you were trying to touch the ceiling with your hands. Rotate your clasped hands in as wide a circle as you can, following with the entire upper body. Make ten circles in the air. Then unclasp hands and lower them to your sides.

4. Raise arms to shoulder level, and clasp hands in front of you, a foot away from your neck. Raise elbows, keeping clasped hands level with the collarbone. Lower elbows as far down as you can, still keeping hands in same position. Inhale while raising, exhale while lowering. Do ten quick repetitions.

5. Stand with feet comfortably apart, arms at sides. Shrug shoulders as high as you can, then let them drop as low as you can. Now rotate head and neck slowly from left to right, attempting to touch left ear to left shoulder, chin to chest, right ear to right shoulder, tilting head as far behind in back as you can. Do ten slow rotations and relax.

6. Stand with feet and legs as far apart as possible while still maintaining balance. Clasp hands behind your neck. Twist torso, and bend as if to touch the right knee with the left elbow (don't worry that they don't touch, just go as close as you can without straining). Rise and return to starting position, and reverse, trying to touch left knee with right elbow. Start with five repetitions and work up to ten.

7. Stand with your feet comfortably apart. Raise your body to its fullest height. Raise your arms up and straight over your head, then slowly curl forward from the fingers down to the base of the

spine, until your hands are hanging down slightly in front of your toes. Keep stomach muscles firm. Rest in this position for a count of twenty. Slowly uncurl to upright position.

The more ambitious can go on to do some push-ups and sit-ups. But these seven will definitely set you up for anything else. Beginning your morning with these exercises, or doing them to break up a long day of little physical activity, will make for a much longer, more enjoyable day.

If you let the attention you pay to the clothing that covers your body be matched by the care you take with what's underneath, it will enhance your appearance and pleasure, and help ensure that you have the relaxed but alert air that is so much a part of the power look.

APPENDIX

Where to Shop for the Power Look

Shopping for the Power Look in London

We all grew up hearing that London is a man's town. It still is. Even today, the British man of style remains a model for most of the world. "Swinging" London came and went, but Savile Row goes on turning out the power look. Buying clothes in London is a luxurious business, and the things you buy there have a character that exports well, no matter where you wear them. The same cannot be said of things you might buy while traveling in much of Europe, or in Africa, South America, or Asia. London is the best place to invest any money you have allotted for clothes, Italy the second best.

TAILORS

A made-to-measure suit from a Savile Row tailor is the ultimate status dressing for many men. You can dress yourself as well or better in ready-made clothing bought at home, but if you still covet—and can afford—a "bespoke" (custom-made) suit, why not?

Huntsman, 11 Savile Row. The firm of H. Huntsman & Sons goes back to 1809 but opened in Savile Row in 1919. They have a great reputation for riding and country clothes in particular. They also make superb city suits in about eight weeks. A two-piece suit, made with about three fittings, costs around £333 (approximately $666).

Henry Poole & Co., Cork Street. Founded in 1801, Poole was the first tailor to open in Savile Row, in 1843. When the company lost its lease in 1961 and moved to nearby Cork Street, its very grand clientele followed. One of the first royals to be dressed by Poole was Napoleon III; another was Emperor Haile Selassie. It is a great favorite with American business royalty, as well. A representative from Poole visits the States twice a year. Write to the London store to find out the itinerary. Prices are slightly lower than at Huntsman, but not much.

Anderson & Sheppard, 30 Savile Row. This is Fred Astaire's tailor. This is also a good address to have if you need a suit with lightning speed; they can make one in a week. The price averages about £200 (about $400).

Kilgour, French & Stanbury, Dover Street. Famous for their workmanship, they have also become famous for their excellent ready-to-wear line sold (at half the price of a made-to-measure garment) across the street in their Number 10 shop.

Pope & Bradley, Dover Street. There is a long tradition of innovation here. They invented the shawl collar in the 1930s and dressed the Duke of Windsor when he was still the Prince of Wales in the 1920s.

Hawes & Curtis, 43 Dover Street. Prince Philip, Prince Charles, Earl Mountbatten, and Cary Grant go here. Starting price for a two-piece suit with three fittings is £175 ($350). It will be ready in a month.

Gieves & Hawkes, 1 Savile Row. They can make a suit for you in forty-eight hours if need be. They take more time on such work as military tailoring for the Queen, uniforms for the Queen's Bodyguard (the Gentlemen-at-Arms), and for officers of the Royal Navy and Army. Town suits are about £190 ($380).

BOOTMAKERS

Style works from the feet up. No matter what else you wear, really superb shoes will lift its quality and character. Custom-made shoes are extravagantly expensive but one of the world's great luxuries, and they can last for more than a lifetime: Lobb has had shoes returned for repair a hundred years after they were made. Forty years is the usual lifespan, though. You don't get that kind of mileage from a car, even a Ferrari.

John Lobb, 9 St. James's Street. They like to see references or have a recommendation from a present customer. There are some 20,000 men whose lasts—the wooden forms that are sculpted to the precise shape of your foot—are stored in the basement, so chances are you might know one. Bill Blass is an American customer; so are Henry Ford and William Paley.

The lasts stay at Lobb so shoes may be made to your order forever, wherever you are. Price for the initial order includes the cost of making the last. Shoes are from £120 ($240) and boots from £200 ($400). They take from two to four months to complete.

Trickers, 67 Jermyn Street. Trickers makes shoes, boots, and those velvet slippers embroidered with the head of a fox or pheasant, the kind that the Rothschild men favor. The price for the first pair of shoes (including the last) is £60 ($120), and subsequent ones about £55 ($110). Slippers are £30 to £35 ($60–$70). It takes about six months to complete your order.

HABERDASHERS

Fine shirts and ties, cashmere sweaters, and custom-made pajamas and dressing gowns are among the glories of British style.

Turnbull & Asser, 71 Jermyn Street. Turnbull & Asser are preeminent for style and for quality. They reinvented the wide tie. They maintain their own silk mill for producing unique designs for shirts and ties. Silk shirts, made-to-measure, are £40 ($80), cotton ones from £16 ($32). They also stock ready-to-wear sweaters, handkerchiefs, pajamas, and robes, as well as shirts.

UMBRELLA MAKERS

James Smith & Sons, 53 New Oxford Street. They maintain a stock of more than a thousand umbrellas at prices up to £16.50 ($33); and they can make one to your specifications. Also found here are walking sticks and canes from £1.50 ($3).

SPORTS AND EVENING WEAR TO HIRE

Traveling light precludes packing a morning suit and top hat, even if you own them. You also probably leave your saddle, riding clothes, fishing tackle, etc., at home. Should you need these or any other regular or sportswear or equipment in England, go to:

Moss Bros., Bedford Street, Covent Garden. Since 1860, this firm has been ready to see Londoners and travelers through spur-of-the-moment needs. Renting clothes at Moss Bros. is a socially correct power ploy, and they will see that they fit as well as your own, so don't worry. Rental of a dinner suit starts at £8 ($16).

Shopping for the Power Look in Paris

In men's clothes, as in automobiles, the French sense of design is different. Just as the Citroën looks unlike cars made in England, Germany, Italy, or the United States, so French menswear seems to reflect a slightly different sensibility. I wouldn't advise any real stocking-up in Paris. For one thing, prices are high. For another, French clothes can look a little far out when worn in most American cities. But have a look—workmanship is often excellent, and colors and fabrics can be beautiful.

"Brummel" in Printemps. Brummel is the multilevel men's annex in the enormous department store Printemps. It's the best place for an overview of the French ready-to-wear possibilities.

Christian Dior Boutique Monsieur, 30 Avenue Montaigne. Ostentatiously luxurious shirts, ties, robes, sweaters, sportswear, etc., are found here.

Hermès. Here is the source for the famous silk scarves and wildly expensive and superb leather goods, from wallets and luggage through the custom-made saddles with which the business began.

Lanvin II, 2 Rue de Cambon. Beautiful shirts, ties, and so on, along with fine tailored clothing are found at Lanvin II, as well as made-to-measure hats by the famous old firm of Gelot, which was acquired by Lanvin.

Renoma, 129 bis, Rue de la Pompe. Youthful and imaginative, Renoma has shirts, pants, sports clothes, blazers, etc., styled to attract the elegant young men of the fashionable 16th arrondissement.

Shopping for the Power Look in Rome

Men in Italy devote more care to their clothes and the way they wear them than do men in any other country. To cater to the Italian's enthusiasm for dressing well, Rome is oversupplied with first-rate shops and stores. Naming the best is almost impossible, because the level of taste and quality is so high everywhere. Try walking along the via Condotti from the foot of the Spanish steps, then turn into the neighboring via Borgognona. You will find dozens of good stores—the internationally famous names such as Gucci and Fendi, along with names famous to Romans and knowledgeable travelers. Explore. That's what the Romans do in Rome.

Some of the best buys are in suedes and leathers, because the skins and the workmanship are top-notch. Clothing, gloves, wallets, luggage, belts, almost anything made from hides is a good bet. But be careful with shoes. Many Americans are unable to get a good fit with Italian lasts. Shirts in silks and fine cottons are another area to look into when shopping in Rome. Fabrics, colors, and patterns are often very beautiful. The same is true of neckties and sweaters.

It is still possible (barely) to afford custom-made shirts and shoes in Rome. The names to remember: for shoes, Gatto, via Salandra, 34; for shirts, Battistoni, via Condotti, 61/a.

Mail-order Shopping for Leisure Clothes

How much money to spend is determined by how much time you spend wearing leisure clothes. But in considering where to buy, you have available some of the world's great sources—no matter where you live—in the great catalog houses such as L. L. Bean of Freeport, Maine.

The places that specialize in really rugged clothing are well worth the trouble of writing to for catalogs. They are specialists, usually, in hunting and fishing gear, as well as in clothes for hiking or other active pursuits. What they sell *has* to work, or they'd soon be out of business. Because these are clothes with a function, fashion is not the first consideration. What you get is handsome, perenially authentic style, whether you wear the clothes for the original use or not.

L. L. Bean & Co., Freeport, Maine 04032. Everything for the outdoors, for hunting, fishing, camping, and so on, is found here. The quality is sturdy, first-rate. Their catalog costs $1.

Miller's, Mail-order Division, Canal Street Station, P.O. Box 720, New York, New York 10013. Miller's carries classic and beautiful English and western riding gear. Their catalog is $1.

Hunting World Inc., 16 East 53rd Street, New York, New York 10022. They carry luxurious hunting and fishing clothes and equipment, with an emphasis on safari. Visit when in New York or send $3 for their catalog.

Fulton Supply Co., 23 Fulton Street, New York, New York 10038. Fulton's has all kinds of gear for the boating and sailing enthusiast.

GLOSSARY

The following is a rundown of descriptive terms for fabrics, fibers, weaves, and so on used in this book and found on clothing labels. Some tips on practical considerations such as cost and durability are also included.

Acetate. A cellulose fiber used, mainly in blends with other fibers, in fabrics for shirts and slacks. Soft, often of high luster, it must usually be dry-cleaned (but follow label instructions). Manufacturer's trade names for acetate include Acele, Celaperm, Estron, and Loftura. (*See also* Cellulose Fibers)

Acrylic. A synthetic fiber used for a wide variety of knits, such as sweaters and knit polo shirts. It's usually soft to the touch and lightweight. Manufacturers' trade names include Acrilan, Creslan, and Orlon. (*See also* Noncellulose Fibers)

Alpaca. A very soft, warm, silky wool woven from hair of the Peruvian alpaca (a relative of the llama) and used primarily for coats. It's very expensive. Part-alpaca blends are also used for suits.

Argyle. A plaid pattern of diamond-shaped blocks crossed by diagonal overstripes of contrasting color. It is used mostly for knits such as socks and sweaters.

Block Print. A small, neat, overall repeat pattern such as is produced by engraved printing blocks. (*See also* Hand-block Printing)

Breech Twill. See Cavalry Twill.

Broadcloth. A finely woven fabric most commonly of cotton but also of wool or silk. Its name comes from the fact that it was the first fabric woven on wide, or broad, looms, as opposed to the narrow looms used for other fabrics. It is closely woven with a very light crosswise rib, similar to poplin but finer. Broadcloth shirts are considered fairly formal.

Camel's Hair. A soft, heavy, luxury wool made entirely or primarily from the hair of the camel. It's almost always found in natural light tan, and it is very warm but doesn't feel weighty. "Camel" alone refers to the color and doesn't mean the wool is of camel's hair. Camel's hair is used primarily for coats and jackets, but also for trousers and knitted sweaters.

Cashmere. The source of cashmere is the downy wool underneath the outer hair of cashmere goats, native to the Himalayas. The yarn is very soft and silky, light but warm. It is also fragile. For strength in coats and jackets, cashmere is often blended before weaving with other, more rugged wools. Pure cashmere makes a beautiful and luxurious coat but is unsuitable for trousers, which are subject to much greater stress in wearing. Cashmere is also the costliest, but warmest and silkiest, wool used in knits. Because of its fragility, the strands of yarn (called "ply") are twisted together for greater strength in knits. Therefore, a three-ply cashmere sweater is more durable, warmer, and more luxurious than a two-ply.

Cavalry Twill. A superstrong ribbed wool cloth formerly used for cavalry officers' uniforms and now used for suits, jackets, and trousers, usually khaki tan or camel in color. It is also called "breech twill," and as the name suggests, it's especially excellent for trousers.

Cellulose Fibers. Man-made, but not synthetic, fibers made from cellulose, the material found in all plants. Major cellulose fibers include acetate, rayon, and triacetate. (*See also* Noncellulose Fibers)

Chalk Stripe. White stripe of the width that would be produced if drawn by a piece of tailor's chalk.

Challis. One of the softest wool weaves, used in shirts, ties, and robes. It is very thin and usually printed with a paisley or small geometric design.

Chambray. A cotton shirting fabric with a frosted effect produced by weaving white threads lengthwise, colored ones (usually blue, ecru, or pink) crosswise. It is a fine variety of gingham and is used for informal shirts.

Cheviot. A wool fabric in a twill weave, similar to serge but rougher and heavier, originally made with wool of cheviot goats. It is a very durable material used for suits, coats, jackets, and trousers. (*See also* Serge)

Chevron Weave. A kind of zigzag herringbone pattern, usually in a solid color (such as white-on-white) but occasionally in two colors.

Chinos. Clothes, usually casual trousers, made of khaki-color cotton twill uniform cloth. Chinos are often referred to as "khakis."

Corduroy. A ribbed cotton fabric used for shirts, jackets, suits, and trousers. Its name comes from the French *cord du roi* or "king's cord," which in France was used for outdoor livery for the royal servants at Versailles. Now worn by kings and everybody else, corduroy is soft and incredibly rugged. Pinwale corduroy is so closely ribbed that it is similar in effect to cotton velvet. In wide-wale corduroy, wales (or ribs) are very broad for greater ruggedness and durability, yet the fabric still has a velvety sheen and softness.

Cotton. Pure cotton is the most comfortable (and coolest in the summertime) fiber for shirts. The finest cotton cloth is that made with the longest staple—the professional term for the natural length of the fiber, which varies from one-quarter inch to about five inches. Egyptian, Sea Island, and Pima cottons have the longest staple. But since polyester fiber can be extruded to indefinite length, polyester-and-cotton blends can result in fine silky cloth from even short-staple cotton. The higher the proportion of natural fibers in blends, the better the cloth will feel when worn (but the more it will rumple).

Covert. In fox hunting, covert means shelter. Hunters often wore clothes of this wool material when "riding to covert"—hence the name. Usually found now in topcoats, covert is identified by a finely speckled surface and diagonal twill weave. It is all wool (or wool and worsted), medium-weight, durable, and sometimes waterproofed.

Crepe de Chine. A soft silk fabric with a finely crinkled surface and subdued luster, used for shirts and pajamas.

Denim. The toughest cotton, used mainly for blue jean trousers but also for informal jackets. The characteristic blue color comes from weaving white crosswise yarns with indigo blue lengthwise yarns. It is also made in many other colors.

Doeskin. A firm, short-nap wool used for blazers and vests. It has the color and softness of the skin of a doe.

Donegal. A homespun Irish tweed, used for suits, jackets, and trousers. Yarns of varying thickness and color produce the identifying spots or nubs on the surface.

Duck. A heavy, tightly woven cotton similar to canvas or sailcloth, used primarily for sports trousers.

Egyptian Cotton. Longest staple cotton, fine and silky, usually found in fine broadcloth shirts. It once came from Egypt but is now grown in the southwestern United States. (*See also* Cotton)

Faille. A silk characterized by a ribbed or corded surface and used for black bow ties.

Flannel. Smooth, dense, somewhat lustrous wool weave with a soft nap and fairly light in weight. Flannel tailors well and is comfortable in almost any weather. But it is very flexible, so it can wrinkle or sag fairly easily. It is used for suits, jackets, and fine trousers. (*See also* Worsted Flannel)

Foulard. Soft, satiny silk with a very fine twill weave. It is usually printed with clear, precise patterns, either allover and large scale, or of regularly spaced small figures. Foulard silk is used for neckties and scarves.

Gabardine. Firm, tightly woven fabric of wool or cotton (or cotton-and-polyester blend) with a pronounced diagonal twill rib. It comes in many weights and makes a durable suit, jacket, or trousers, though it may eventually get shiny at friction points.

Gingham Checks. Small, even checks, usually in one light and one darker shade of the same color over white.

Glen Check. Small, even check pattern used in tweeds. It is usually in two colors.

Glenurquhart. A Scottish clan tartan often found in worsted suitings. The original tartan is black and white, although it is now often made in many other combinations of two muted colors. The design has squares of small woven checks alternating with squares of larger checks.

Grosgrain. Ribbed or corded-surface silk used for black bow ties. It is similar to faille, but the ribs are heavier and rounder.

Gun Club Check. Tweed design in which a large check is woven over a smaller check.

Hairline Stripe. An extremely narrow stripe, about the width of a hair.

Hand-block Printing. The most expensive way of getting a pattern onto silk (or any other material). Paste dyes are applied to carved or engraved blocks of wood or metal and pressed against the fabric.

Harris Tweed. A wool handwoven on the island of Harris, off the coast of Scotland. Soft wool yarns are dyed before weaving, and varying colors are combined for muted colorings (called heather shades) which suggest the colors of local plants and flowers. Harris tweed is found in suits, jackets, trousers, and coats.

Herringbone. A zigzag woven pattern suggesting the skeleton of a fish. Rows of chevron stripes are woven in two close or contrasting colors to form a herringbone pattern.

Homespun. Plain wool weave, but often of luxury fibers such as cashmere or mohair blended with other wool. It is used for blazers and jackets and occasionally trousers. It has a tendency to sag unless tightly woven.

Hopsacking. Plain, somewhat coarse weave of wool resembling sackcloth, used for jackets, suits, and trousers.

Houndstooth Check. A small, irregular design of broken checks. To the English-speaking, the pattern's checks resemble canine teeth; the French call it *pied-de-poule* ("chicken's foot").

Jacquard Weave. A figured knit or woven fabric produced by a special Jacquard loom. Intricate designs in two or more colors can be produced with this weave. In men's clothing, it is used primarily for sweaters with elaborate color and pattern.

Lamb's Wool. Very soft wool, shorn from lambs younger than eight months old. It makes a soft, luxurious sweater.

Linen. A fine, textured, strong cloth made of flax. Because it sags and wrinkles so easily, today it is rarely found pure; often it is blended with man-made fibers for longer-lasting shape.

Loden. Very thick, blanketlike wool from Austria, used for coats. It has a natural water-shedding quality and is very warm. It usually comes in deep forest green, but also in gray and occasionally other colors.

Macclesfield. Rather rough-textured silk used for ties and scarves, usually in a solid color, with small, allover pattern woven in. It is also called Spitalfield.

Madras. Lightweight cotton from India, usually in multicolored plaid prints, used for shirts, ties, jackets, and trousers. "Bleeding" madras is intended to run and fade in washing; the result is a softer, subtler coloration. End-on-end madras is a plain-color cotton with a frosted or muted effect produced by weaving together white "end" (or lengthwise) threads with pastel-colored crosswise ones; the result is similar to chambray.

Melton. Like a very thick felt, made of pure wool or wool and cotton. Its deep nap is usually shorn to show the basic twill weave. Used for warm overcoats, primarily in dark blue or grayish tan.

Merino. Extremely fine wool, similar to cashmere, from a breed of Spanish sheep. It's used for sweaters.

Modacrylic. A noncellulose fiber used in deep-pile and synthetic fur cloths for trimming or lining coats. It holds up well, but it must usually be dry-cleaned. It is also known by the manufacturer's trade name of Dynel. (*See also* Noncellulose Fibers)

Mogador. Brightly striped silk with a strong ribbed or corded face, used for ties and scarves.

Mohair. Fine, silky wool from Angora goats. In sweaters, it is generally combined with other wool for knits with a shaggy look.

Moiré. A silk fabric also known as watered silk because of the wavy, irregular pattern pressed into the face of the material. Its best use is for black or white suspenders for wear with a dinner suit; vests are also made of moiré, but these look fussy.

Noncellulose Fibers. Synthetic fibers made from coal, salt, and petroleum (as opposed to cellulose fibers, which are made of plant material). The main types are acrylic, modacrylic, nylon, polyester, and olefin. (*See also* Cellulose Fibers)

Olefin. A noncellulose fiber, used for lightweight knit shirts, sweaters, socks. The fiber allows perspiration to reach the surface of the fabric and evaporate. Most other synthetics tend to trap moisture inside, so garments made of them are hotter to wear than those made of olefin. Major manufacturers' trade names are Herculon and Marvess. (*See also* Noncellulose Fibers)

Oxford Cloth. Cotton fabric with small basketweave surface, used for shirts. It is soft and comfortable, but it frays at friction points (collars and cuffs). Usually it comes in white, pastel shades, or colored stripes on white. Less lustrous than broadcloth, it is also considered slightly less formal.

Pima Cotton. High-grade, very strong medium-staple cotton developed in Pima County, Arizona, and used for fine broadcloth shirts. (*See also* Cotton)

Pincord. A cotton cord fabric with very narrow ribs. Colors are usually pale blue, gray, or tan with white. It is used for summer suitings.

Pinstripe. A very fine stripe, less than one-sixteenth of an inch.

Polyester. A noncellulose fiber used in every clothing category. Pure polyester or blends of polyester and wool are found in suits, jackets, and trousers. Pure polyester may have a stiff, shiny look. But blended with wool, it can produce a fabric with superior warmth and resilience. Manufacturers' trade names include Avlin, Dacron, Encron, Fortrel, Kodel, Trevira, and Vycron. (*See also* Noncellulose Fibers)

Poplin. A cotton material similar to broadcloth, but heavier and with a more pronounced rib. It is firm, durable, and popular for warm-weather suits.

Prince of Wales Plaid. A bold, crisp tweed pattern, similar to a Glenurquhart plaid, favored by the late Duke of Windsor in the 1920s when he was Prince of Wales.

Rayon. A cellulose fiber used for ties and lining cloths. It is valued for its natural sheen and softness, and for the ease of dyeing. Treated to reduce its luster, rayon may also be blended with polyester for tailored clothing. Manufacturers' trade names include Arvil, Enka, and Zantrel. (*See also* Cellulose Fibers)

Regimental Stripe. A rep silk with the colors and width of stripes of a British regiment tie. (*See also* Rep)

Rep. A silk woven with fine crosswise ribs, used for neckties. Rep silks are usually patterned with woven stripes, although they may also be of solid color. The silk is cut and sewn on the bias (or at an angle) so the stripes run on the diagonal when made into a tie.

Sanforized. Trade name for a process applied to cotton to reduce the possibility of shrinkage.

Satin. A smooth basic weave, usually of silk. Silk satin is very formal and elegant. Used to face lapels of a dinner jacket, a narrow satin strip also covers the side seam of the trousers. The bow tie may be of satin, too. Silk satin demands careful treatment. Water spots it, and a fingernails can snag it beyond repair. Satins made of such synthetic fiber as Qiana nylon are equally good-looking but easier to live with.

Scottish District Check Tweed. Any of several small-scale check patterns traditionally identified with various areas of Scotland.

Sea Island Cotton. One of the finest long-staple cottons, found in top-quality shirtings. It once came from Sea Island and other islands off the Georgia and South Carolina coast, but it's now grown in other regions of the United States. (*See also* Cotton)

Seersucker. Thin, lightweight fabric marked by alternating smooth and crinkled stripes woven in. It is seen most frequently in blue, gray, or brown stripes on white. Seersucker can also be solid-color or printed. Originally pure cotton, it is now usually made of blends, occasionally of silk.

Serge. Twill weave with a flat, diagonal rib that shows on the front and back of the fabric. It is a durable fabric used for suits, trousers, and jackets, but its surface eventually becomes shiny from wear. Wide-wale serge (also called cheviot serge) has a more pronounced diagonal rib and is heavier and rougher to the touch.

Shearling. A garment, usually a jacket or coat, made from the skins of lambs or sheep from which the short-wooled fleece has not been removed. Hides are tanned with the wool on, and the garment is made so that the wool side is worn next to the body and serves as a lining for the coat.

Shetland. Wool from the Shetland Island sheep, woven into a fine tweed for suits, jackets, and trousers, or knitted into dense, fuzzy sweaters.

Silk. A fine, soft, shiny fabric made from fibers produced by silkworms as they form their cocoons. It is a luxurious fabric, standard for fine neckties; scarves, evening shirts, robes, pajamas, and even suits are also made of silk. If too shiny, silk can look cheap. The lower the luster, the better; a dull-finish silk always looks richer. For a silk suit, a silk poplin in natural ecru is beautiful. Darker colors reflect light more and look shinier.

Spitalfield. See Macclesfield.

Tattersall Check. A traditional check pattern of two sets of dark lines in a regularly spaced check design on a light ground. The classic coloring is red-and-black on cream, although many other colorings are found today. Blankets in this pattern were used on horses in the London market founded by Richard Tattersall in 1766. It soon became a popular material for vests for sportsmen and is now popular for shirting cloths.

Triacetate. A cellulose fiber used for sport shirts, and in blends with other fibers, for tailored clothing. It is amazingly resistant to wrinkling and often machine-washable. Major manufacturer's trade name is Arnel. (*See also* Cellulose Fibers)

Tropical Worsted. Lightweight summer suiting made of worsted (twisted) wool alone or blended with other fibers. It tailors and holds its shape well.

Tweed. A rough-surfaced wool fabric of two or more colors. The name is derived from "tweeled," a Scottish variation of "twilled," meaning twisted. Wools are dyed before weaving; usually shades of several different colors are woven together for muted, heather colorings or for check, plaid, or herringbone patterns. The rough surface is the result of using irregular threads. It is one of the most durable and handsome of all fabrics, used for suits, jackets, trousers, and coats.

Twist. A woolen or worsted fabric with a tight, sturdy finish. It is often woven of two twisted-together yarns of varying shades to produce a slightly mottled effect.

Unfinished Worsted. A wool weave used for suits, jackets, and trousers. Because the slight nap is not clipped after weaving, the pattern of the weave is less obvious than in most worsteds, yet not as obscure as in flannel or melton.

Velvet. A rich fabric of silk or cotton, or blends of part silk or cotton, with a soft, thick pile. Silk velvet is sturdy enough for an evening bow tie, and quite beautiful; but for a velvet dinner suit, cotton velvet is quieter in effect and sturdier. Suits of velvet should not be tailored too tightly as they can easily rip and are difficult to mend.

Velveteen. A cotton cloth stronger than velvet, though not quite so soft or plush. It makes a better fabric for such things as "velvet" jeans.

Virgin Wool. Any wool that has not been used before, from the first shearing of the sheep. It is used for sweaters.

Viyella. Trade name for a twill-weave flannel of wool-and-cotton yarns, blended before spinning and woven into a very soft, warm, lightweight cloth used primarily for shirts.

Voile. A plain, sheer fabric. For menswear, it is usually made of cotton and used for shirts and handkerchiefs.

Watered Silk. See Moiré.

Whipcord. Tightly woven wool worsted with strong diagonal ribs or cords, similar to gabardine but with ribbing heavier and wider (up to one-eighth of an inch). Very handsome and practical for trousers, it is also used for jackets and suits.

Windowpane Check. A plain, barred plaid like the pattern of panes and mullions in a window.

Wind-tab Buttonholes. A device allowing the lapel of a jacket to be buttoned over the chest and throat as protection from cold weather. It consists of a button on one lapel and a loop, or tab, sewn to the outer edge of the facing lapel.

Worsted. Very smooth-surfaced wool fabric woven of worsted (twisted) yarn spun from long-staple, evenly combed wool. The wool is tightly twisted before weaving for strength and resilience. Gabardine, serge, and worsted flannel are examples. The name comes from the town of Worstead, England, where a particularly fine woolen cloth originated.

Worsted Flannel. Like flannel, but more durable. It has a flatter finish and shows a more pronounced diagonal pattern in the weave. (*See also* Flannel)

INDEX